Selected Poems

of

John Donne

Crofts Classics

GENERAL EDITORS

Samuel H. Beer, *Harvard University*

O. B. Hardison, Jr., *The Folger Shakespeare Library*

John Simon

On the cover is reproduced a wood engraving of an alchemist in his laboratory. Note the sun and the moon, symbols of gold and silver, while below them is the sign for mercury. The lion devouring the snake represents an acid dissolving a salt. Alchemy, together with more soundly based science, provided Donne with some of his "metaphysical" imagery.

Research for cover art by Nigel Foxell.

JOHN DONNE

Selected Poems

EDITED BY

M. A. Shaaber

UNIVERSITY OF PENNSYLVANIA

AHM PUBLISHING CORPORATION
Northbrook, Illinois 60062

ISBN: 0-88295-032-0

(Formerly 390-22345-X)

Library of Congress Card Number: 58-12942

PRINTED IN THE UNITED STATES OF AMERICA

733

FOURTEENTH PRINTING

contents

Elegies

Satires

Letters to Several Personages

introduction

The poems of Donne printed below are classified according to the scheme adopted in the edition of 1635. They might be more simply divided into two classes, secular and religious, but it is well to separate such groups as the love poems, the satires, and the occasional poems because of significant differences of matter and manner. The satires are satires after the Renaissance fashion, i.e., poems in which bad morals or bad manners are dismissed with loathing or contempt, though the specimen printed here transcends some of the limitations of the genre. The occasional poems (meagerly represented in this selection) are exhibitions of the poet's wit. He writes to friends like Sir Henry Wotton or Christopher Brooke to amuse them and compliment them, not least by implying that they and he belong, in morals and in sensibility, to a superior class; he writes to noble ladies like the Countesses of Bedford and Huntingdon to flatter them with extravagant imputations of beauty and virtue and with even more extravagant self-abasement. The funeral elegies, ostensibly poems of religious meditation and consolation, also partake of the nature of occasional poetry since Donne usually wrote them for and presented them to bereaved survivors.

Donne's popularity, however, depends on the love poems and the religious poems. The love poems (the "songs and sonnets" and the elegies) are mostly monologues spoken by a lover to a woman (usually an inamorata, but in a few poems a woman more distantly and respectfully admired) or to the god of love himself or occasionally to a third person. The first thing about them that strikes the reader is their bewildering variety of tone and mood, ranging from utter cynicism about love ("Oh, 'tis imposture all!") to exultation in a love fully reciprocated and the fervent celebration of it as "all spirit, pure and brave." Each poem stands on its own legs, of course, but it is also part of a protracted examination of love which has the additional interest of exposing its depths and its heights, its vagaries and its contradictions.

The lover of these poems is not the usual passionate adorer of a beautiful woman or the lamenting victim of her coldness. The poems are full of passion, but it is not a sensual yearning for the fulfillment of love so much as the passion of resentment or defiance, as often directed against love itself as against a recalcitrant mistress. The lover vacillates between accepting and rejecting love. Some poems reflect love as "peace" but more as "rage"; in both kinds the other aspect is never far away. Similarly in the poems in which the inconstancy of women is expatiated on or assumed, the thought of "correspondency" in love lurks about too, and a rueful recollection of woman's frailty sometimes obtrudes upon the poems of rapture and even of compliment. There is a curious detachment about the speaker of these poems for all the strength of his anger and his pride: he tells us not how he feels, being in love, but what he thinks about the experience, how he puzzles his head over it, how he tries to explain it to himself. Almost every poem is a quizzical examination of some aspect of love or some kind of relationship between man and woman. Broadly speaking, the question is "what is love?" —especially, is it of the flesh or of the spirit? Thus the poems strive for an intellectual rather than an emotional apprehension of love, often enough in a perfect fury of disdain or bafflement or in a burst of pride. No real conclusion is reached: Donne, or at any rate the speaker of the poems, remains of at least two minds about women, honor, love, himself.

The detachment is evident, moreover, in the humorous flavor which inheres in even the most equable of them. The humor of jeux d'esprit like "The Will" and "The Flea" is obvious, but it may well be suspected that many another was written with tongue in cheek, and a measure of humorous or playful exaggeration can be detected in all. "The Sun Rising" is a wonderful expression of the exultation of the satisfied lover; at the same time the characterization of the sun as a "busy old fool" and a "saucy, pedantic wretch," the supposition that he is blind because the lady's eyes have dazzled his or that he is old and therefore may be excused from some of his work are strokes of humor, and there are overtones of humor in the hyperboles which abound in the poem. The levity of the poems combines with seriousness in volatile combinations to give them much of their perpetual fascination.

Donne's real originality is to be found in his technical virtuosity, his unique manner and style, his wit (to use the inclusive seventeenth-century term). Donne's wit is not chiefly verbal, like that of many of his predecessors or what is called wit today, but achieves surprise and shock by means of bold and ingenious conceptions. The conceit of lovers' exchanging hearts, for example, is common enough in earlier love poetry, but Donne treats it not as a metaphor but as a fact and in a poem like "The Legacy" pushes the conception to extraordinary lengths. The idea that the parting of lovers is a kind of death is boldly assumed to be literally true; the shock is perhaps due chiefly to the fact that Donne does not try to make it acceptable but simply leaves no alternative to accepting it. In many poems some proposition about love—often enough drastic and extravagant—is stated and elaborated by means of ingenious hyperboles. In the first stanza of "The Good-Morrow," a cliché, "we never really lived till we fell in love," is converted into a series of abrupt and fundamentally preposterous questions: what in the world did we do? did we live like stupid peasants? or did we sleep the time away, like the seven sleepers? In "A Valediction: of the Book" the letters the lover and the lady have exchanged become their annals, then the articles of the religion of love, the service books of love's clergy, an encyclopedia of all knowledge sufficient to preserve learning from a new barbarian invasion, law-books specifying the rights of lovers, statesmen's manuals—all these characterizations serving to illustrate the theme of the omnipotence of love. "Confined Love" supports its thesis that the ordinance limiting a woman to the love of one man is unnatural by means of analogies—the universal light of the heavenly bodies, the mating habits of birds and beasts, the unselective utility of ships and real property. Often the theme is developed by ingenious argument, the appearance of close logical thinking. In "Lovers' Infiniteness" the three stanzas start from three different premises about how much of the lady's love the lover has—"If yet I have not all thy love," "if then thou gavest me all," "I would not have all yet." "Community" starts from the assumption that women are neither good nor bad but "things indifferent," to reach, with every appearance of plausibility, its bitter conclusion. The fertile ingenuity and bold directness of such strategies as these delight, tease, and provoke the reader today as much as they did those contemporaries who awarded Donne the laurel of wit.

Another peculiarity of these poems is a certain aridity of tone: rarely has love been considered so abstractly, with so little apparent interest in its sensuous manifestations. For example, of all the inventory of women's beauty on which love poets usually dwell ecstatically, the only items often mentioned by Donne are the eyes and cheeks and these almost exclusively as the source and channel of tears. Nearly everything else is spoken of with the same minimum sensuous excitement: here a ship is no golden galleon but a trading vessel; spring is a season that may be nipped by cold; a flower is something the number of whose petals may have an esoteric meaning. This dry concreteness is all the more remarkable because Donne is extremely fertile in metaphors, comparisons, and analogies. Some poems (like "A Lecture upon the Shadow") pursue a single comparison from beginning to end; others shift from one image to another as they develop. The images themselves are often surprising, yet surprisingly apt; what is illustrated is as a rule widely disparate from the illustration. Uselessness is illustrated by "a sundial in a grave" ("The Will"), love's unremitting growth is compared to the new taxes which princes are granted in time of danger and do not forgo at the return of peace ("Love's Growth"), a casual lover is like a falconer who flies his hawk at any game he fancies and, when the sport is over, turns his thoughts elsewhere ("Love's Diet"), the boredom that ensues upon the lover's conquests is like a child's quickly forgetting the toy he coveted ("Farewell to Love"). Some of his favorite images (the indestructibility of matter, the microcosm, the waters above the firmament, the elixir of life) are a bit recherché and, drawn as they are from his familiarity with philosophical speculation, have often been classified as learned. It was presumably this abstruseness which led Dryden to complain that Donne "affects the metaphysics" and thus to affix the epithet "metaphysical" to his style forever.

Just as Donne plays down the potential sensuousness of

his subject and his images, he also forgoes some of the sensuousness of which verse is capable. His versification is peculiarly his own, especially in the songs and sonnets. Almost every poem has a unique stanza-pattern, never used before and never repeated. These stanzas are often nicely adjusted to the rhetoric of the units they form. Moreover, the rhythm of the lines has little of the "linked sweetness" so abundantly exemplified by English poetry during Donne's youth and maturity. The exceptionally easy tripping movement of "Go and catch a falling star" serves to underscore its flippancy. As a rule Donne is "harsh" (to use his own word), i.e., he prefers a slow and emphatic to a smooth and obviously melodious rhythm. He uses elision freely and his lines therefore often seem densely packed. He will impose a rhetorical emphasis on the iambic movement of the line which seems to be a violent wrenching of the basic rhythm ("Did us to us at first convey," "Coming and staying showed thee, thee"); the effect is startling condensation. The rugged power of many lines and stanzas, by contrast with the mellifluousness of the style of poems of "whining" love, suits very well the rebellious and peremptory attitude of the speaker of the poems and is another cause of their astonishing effect.

The striking effect of Donne's poems is in part the result of their being conceived as miniature dramas. Many of them imply some interplay between the speaker and another person—the lover and his mistress or a monitory friend; the person addressed—mistress, friend, the god of love, or whoever—is always clearly identified and insistently lectured or argued with or cajoled; the interlocutor cannot reply, but his attitude is sometimes skillfully suggested and the tension between him and the speaker is almost always felt. Sometimes changes of the speaker's attitude between stanzas imply a kind of dramatic development. The dynamic imagery, which often evokes a sense of things in motion, in tension, or at strife, intensifies this effect. This technique, of which few poets have held the secret as completely as Donne, makes the poems seem strenuous, alive, dramatic beyond the ordinary. Even those poems in which this quasi-dramatic technique is not conspicuous are enlivened by a flavor of paradox, of opposed ideas and concepts in unresolved tension. The fundamental oppositions of flesh and spirit, of love as peace and love as rage are the substance of many poems and are implied in nearly all the rest (just as the religious poems oppose man lost to man saved or God's condemnation of man to his forgiveness). This strenuousness arises from the argumentative cast of the poems. They abound in clauses beginning with such conjunctions as for, as, if, and since; the speaker is almost always carrying on a debate with someone else or with himself or scrutinizing the reason or unreason of the relationship under consideration. The reasoning is sometimes specious rather than logically impeccable, for Donne, like a resourceful lawyer, can make an impressive argument from any brief, but the dialectical cut and thrust imparts energy and suspense to the poem.

The religious poems are surprisingly like the songs and sonnets. To the elementary premises of Christian teaching Donne applies the shock technique of the love poems. Since the bravura of this technique may be thought less congruous with devotion than with a skeptical attitude toward profane love, the religious poems are perhaps less successful. But the great paradoxes of human life as religious faith conceives it admit of Donne's mode of exploitation as well as the paradoxes and vagaries of mortal love. Man's special status as the creature of God and the inescapable curse of congenital sinfulness, man's wallowing in sin and his desperate anxiety to escape from its toils, the certainty of grisly death and the possibility of escaping from it into eternal life—these fateful anomalies are elaborated with the old wit and a new intensity due to the fact that here, at any rate, the author knows where he stands. The two "anniversaries" (which are religious poems by virtue of their themes—those of traditional religious meditation—if for no other reason), taking the death of a young girl as their text, expatiate on "the frailty and the decay of this whole world" and "the incommodities of the soul in this life and her exaltation in the next" with drastic insight and concentration. A naïve criticism sometimes discounts the religious poems on the assumption that if the love poems are sincere these must be insincere. This is a very shallow conception of sincerity as well as a naïve opinion of the relation of sincerity to poetry. Besides, the writhing sinner who speaks in the religious poems is at least as much humanity in general as Donne individually and personally, just as the rebellious lover of the songs and sonnets may well be a pose which it was convenient for Donne to adopt as much as a self-portrait. Donne the religious poet is almost always the homilist.

The value of Donne's wry scrutiny of love and lovers may be questioned; certainly he is no seer, no mentor, no prophet. The religious poems may seem too strenuous to those whose religion is passive. But if Donne's poems are not asked to deliver immutable truths and are relished simply as poems, they will yield a strangely rich and varied delight. Few poems by any poet afford the reader a more vivid and exciting experience while he is reading them.

principal dates in the life of John Donne

1572   Born in London (probably early in the year).

1576   His father died; his mother presently remarried.

1584 (23 October)   Matriculated from Hart Hall, Oxford.

1590–1591?   Traveled abroad.

1592 (6 May)   Admitted to Lincoln's Inn.

1593   His brother Henry died in prison.

1596 (June)   Served with the Earl of Essex in his raid on Cadiz.

1597 (August)   Served in the Islands voyage, a naval expedition to the Azores which attempted to capture the Spanish silver fleet from America.

1598–1602   Secretary to Sir Thomas Egerton, lord keeper.

1601 (December)   Secretly married Anne More.

1602 (February)   Imprisoned on charges brought by his father-in-law.

1602 (April)   Marriage validated.

1602–1604   Lived at Pyrford with Sir Francis Wooley (his wife's cousin).

1605–1611   Lived at Mitcham.

1610   Published *Pseudo-martyr*.

1610 (17 April)   Created M.A. at Oxford.

1611   Published *Ignatius his conclave*.

1611   Published *An Anatomy of the World* (*The First Anniversarie*).

1611 (November)–1612 (September)   Traveled on the continent with Sir Robert Drury.

1612–1621   Lived in a house off Drury Lane, close to Drury House, the London residence of Sir Robert Drury.

1612   Published *Of the Progres of the Soule* (*The Second Anniversarie*).

1614   M.P. for Taunton.

1615 (23 January)   Ordained.

1615 (April)   Created D.D. at Cambridge.

1617–1622   Reader in divinity at Lincoln's Inn.

1617 (15 August)   His wife died a week after giving birth to her twelfth child.

1619–1620   Accompanied the Viscount Doncaster on an embassy to Germany.

1621 (19 November)   Appointed dean of St. Paul's Cathedral.

1624   Instituted vicar of St. Dunstan's in the West, Fleet St., London.

1624   Published *Devotions upon Emergent Occasions*, written at the end of a severe illness during the preceding winter.

1631 (12 February)   Preached his last sermon.

1631 (31 March)   Died.

1633   *Poems* first published.

SONGS AND SONNETS

Song

Go and catch a falling star,
   Get with child a mandrake root,
Tell me where all past years are,
   Or who cleft the devil's foot,
Teach me to hear mermaids singing,   5
Or to keep off envy's stinging,
        And find
        What wind
Serves to advance an honest mind.

If thou be'st born to strange sights,   10
   Things invisible to see,
Ride ten thousand days and nights
   Till age snow white hairs on thee;
Thou, when thou return'st, wilt tell me
All strange wonders that befell thee,   15
        And swear
        Nowhere
Lives a woman true, and fair.

Songs and sonnets In the 1635 edition, the first to bring them together in a group, the songs and sonnets are printed in an order for which no explanation has ever been found. Since this order, by placing side by side poems flagrantly discordant in tone and mood, has often puzzled readers, it is abandoned here. Instead the poems appear in a sequence which attempts to bring together homogeneous poems and to separate the incongruous. This arrangement implies nothing whatever about the order in which the poems were written, about any presumptive development of Donne's philosophy or understanding of love, or about anything else. **sonnets** poems of love (not necessarily 14-line poems) **2 mandrake root** to which, because of its resemblance to the human body, human properties were attributed **5 mermaids** *i.e.*, sirens

1

If thou find'st one, let me know;
20   Such a pilgrimage were sweet.
Yet do not; I would not go
     Though at next door we might meet.
Though she were true when you met her,
And last till you write your letter,
25   Yet she
               Will be
False, ere I come, to two or three.

Community

Good we must love, and must hate ill,
For ill is ill, and good good still;
     But there are things indifferent
Which we may neither hate nor love,
5   But one and then another prove
     As we shall find our fancy bent.

If then at first wise nature had
Made women either good or bad,
     Then some we might hate and some choose;
10   But since she did them so create
That we may neither love nor hate,
     Only this rests: all, all may use.

If they were good, it would be seen
(Good is as visible as green,
15   And to all eyes itself betrays);
If they were bad, they could not last
(Bad doth itself and others waste);
     So they deserve nor blame nor praise.

But they are ours as fruits are ours:
20   He that but tastes, he that devours,
     And he that leaves all doth as well.
Changed loves are but changed sorts of meat,

---

2 **still** always 3 **indifferent** neutral, neither good nor bad
5 **prove** try out, make use of 12 **rests** remains 21 **as well**
equally well

And when he hath the kernel eat,
Who doth not fling away the shell?

Love's Alchemy

Some that have deeper digged love's mine than I,
Say where his centric happiness doth lie.
    I have loved, and got, and told,
But should I love, get, tell till I were old,
I should not find that hidden mystery.   5
        Oh, 'tis imposture all!
And as no chemic yet the elixir got,
    But glorifies his pregnant pot
    If by the way to him befall
Some odoriferous thing, or med'cinal,   10
    So lovers dream a rich and long delight,
    But get a winter-seeming summer's night.

Our ease, our thrift, our honor, and our day,
Shall we for this vain bubble's shadow pay?
    Ends love in this, that my man   15
Can be as happy as I can, if he can
Endure the short scorn of a bridegroom's play?
    That loving wretch that swears
'Tis not the bodies marry, but the minds
    (Which he in her angelic finds)   20
    Would swear as justly that he hears,
In that day's rude, hoarse minstrelsy, the spheres.
    Hope not for mind in women. At their best
    Sweetness and wit, they're but mummy possessed.

7 **chemic** alchemist   **elixir** *i.e.*, the elixir vitæ, curing all diseases and prolonging life, supposed to be attainable by alchemical processes   8 **pregnant** fruitful   15 **man** manservant   22 **minstrelsy** street songs   **spheres** *i.e.*, the music of the spheres   24 **mummy** dead flesh   **possessed** animated, controlled by a spirit or demon

The Apparition

When by thy scorn, O murd'ress, I am dead,
    And that thou think'st thee free
    From all solicitatión from me,
Then shall my ghost come to thy bed,
5   And thee, feigned vestal, in worse arms shall see.
Then thy sick taper will begin to wink,
    And he whose thou art then, being tired before,
Will, if thou stir or pinch to wake him, think
    Thou call'st for more,
10 And in false sleep will from thee shrink,
And then, poor aspen wretch, neglected, thou
    Bathed in a cold, quicksilver sweat wilt lie
    A verier ghost than I.
What I will say, I will not tell thee now,
15 Lest that preserve thee; and since my love is spent,
I had rather thou shouldst painfully repent
Than by my threat'nings rest still innocent.

The Curse

Whoever guesses, thinks, or dreams he knows
Who is my mistress, wither by this curse:
    His only, and only his purse
    May some dull heart to love dispose,
5 And she yield then to all that are his foes;
    May he be scorned by one whom all else scorn,
    Forswear to others what to her he hath sworn,
    With fear of missing, shame of getting, torn.

Madness his sorrow, gout his cramp, may he
10 Make by but thinking who hath made him such;
    And may he feel no touch

2 **that** when   5 **vestal** virgin   6 **wink** flicker out (because of
the presence of a ghost)   17 **rest** remain 3-4 may his one and
only purse, and nothing but his purse, make some stupid
woman love him

Of conscience, but of fame, and be
Anguished, not that 'twas sin, but that 'twas she.
  In early and long scarceness may he rot
  For land which had been his if he had not   15
  Himself incestuously an heir begot.

May he dream treason and believe that he
Meant to perform it, and confess, and die,
      And no recórd tell why;
      His sons, which none of his may be,   20
Inherit nothing but his infamy;
  Or may he so long parasites have fed
  That he would fain be theirs whom he hath bred,
  And at the last be circumcised for bread.

The venom of all stepdames, gamesters' gall,   25
What tyrants and their subjects interwish,
      What plants, mines, beasts, fowl, fish
      Can cóntribute, all ill which all
Prophets or poets spake, and all which shall
  Be annexed in schedules unto this by me   30
  Fall on that man—for if it be a she,
  Nature beforehand hath outcursèd me.

Woman's Constancy

Now thou hast loved me one whole day,
Tomorrow when thou leav'st, what wilt thou say?
Wilt thou then antedate some new-made vow?
      Or say that now
We are not just those persons which we were?   5
Or that oaths made in reverential fear
Of Love and his wrath, any may forswear?
Or, as true deaths true marriages untie,
So lovers' contracts, images of those,

12 **fame** report, public knowledge   15 **For** for lack of   23
fain be obliged to   **theirs** *i.e.*, the parasite of those   **bred** supported   24 **circumcised** hard up   30 **schedules** supplementary statements   2 **leav'st** stop (loving)   3 **antedate** assign to an earlier date   8 **true** real

10 Bind but till sleep, death's image, them unloose?
            Or, your own end to justify,
    For having purposed change and falsehood, you
    Can have no way but falsehood to be true?
    Vain lunatic, against these scapes I could
15   Dispute and conquer, if I would,
               Which I abstain to do,
    For by tomorrow I may think so too.

The Legacy

    When I died last (and, dear, I die
        As often as from thee I go,
        Though it be but an hour ago,
    And lovers' hours be full eternity)
5   I can remember yet that I
        Something did say and something did bestow
    (Though I be dead) which sent me I should be
    Mine own executor and legacy.

    I heard me say, "Tell her anon
10   That myself (that's you, not I)
        Did kill me, and when I felt me die,
    I bid me send my heart when I was gone."
    But I, alas, could there find none
        When I had ripped me and searched where
                        hearts did lie.
15 It killed me again that I who still was true
    In life, in my last will should cozen you.

    Yet I found something like a heart,
        But colors it, and corners, had;
        It was not good, it was not bad,
20 It was entire to none, and few had part.
    As good as could be made by art

14 **Vain** ineffectual **lunatic** (1) madwoman, (2) changeable
woman **scapes** evasions 17 **think so** *i.e.*, love you no longer
7 **sent me** brought it about, ordained 15 **still** always 16
cozen cheat 18 **colors . . . had** was painted, deceptive
corners had *i.e.*, was imperfect 20 **entire to** exclusively pos-
sessed by

It seemed; and therefore, for our losses sad,
I meant to send this heart instead of mine,
But oh, no man could hold it, for 'twas thine.

The Message

Send home my long-strayed eyes to me,
Which oh too long have dwelt on thee;
Yet since there they have learned such ill,
   Such forced fashions
   And false passions   5
     That they be
     Made by thee
Fit for no good sight, keep them still.

Send home my harmless heart again,
Which no unworthy thought could stain;   10
But if it be taught by thine
   To make jestings
   Of protestings,
    And cross both
    Word and oath,   15
Keep it, for then 'tis none of mine.

Yet send me back my heart and eyes
That I may know and see thy lies,
And may laugh and joy when thou
   Art in anguish   20
   And dost languish
    For some one
    That will none,
Or prove as false as thou art now.

Love's Usury

For every hour that thou wilt spare me now,
    I will allow,
Usurious god of love, twenty to thee,

4 forced fashions artificial behavior   **14 cross** cross out, cancel
23 *i.e.*, that will have none of you

When with my brown my grey hairs equal be.
5   Till then, Love, let my body reign, and let
Me travel, sojourn, snatch, plot, have, forget,
Resume my last year's relict, think that yet
               We had never met.

Let me think any rival's letter mine,
10   And at next nine
Keep midnight's promise; mistake by the way
The maid, and tell the lady of that delay.
Only let me love none—no, not the sport.
From country grass to comfitures of court
15   Or city's *quelque-choses* let report
               My mind transport.

This bargain's good: if when I'm old I be
               Inflamed by thee,
If thine own honor, or my shame or pain,
20   Thou covet, most at that age thou shalt gain.
Do thy will then; then subject and degree
And fruit of love, Love, I submit to thee.
Spare me till then, I'll bear it, though she be
               One that loves me.

The Indifferent

I can love both fair and brown,
Her whom abundance melts, and her whom want betrays,
Her who loves loneness best, and her who masks and
               plays,
Her whom the country formed, and whom the town,
5   Her who believes, and her who tries,
       Her who still weeps with spongy eyes,
       And her who is dry cork and never cries;

7 **relict** that which I left   10 **nine** nine o'clock   11 **mistake**
(1) take by mistake, (2) take wrongfully   14 **comfitures** con-
fectionary   15 *quelque-choses* (literally) fancy dishes   21
subject whom I shall love   **degree** how much I shall love   22
fruit what shall come of my loving   **submit to thee** resign to
your direction   5 **tries** examines (all beliefs)

I can love her, and her, and you, and you;
I can love any, so she be not true.

Will no other vice content you? 10
Will it not serve your turn to do as did your mothers?
Or have you all old vices spent, and now would find out
          others?
  Or doth a fear that men are true torment you?
    O, we are not; be not you so.
    Let me, and do you, twenty know. 15
    Rob me, but bind me not, and let me go.
Must I, who came to travail thorough you,
Grow your fixed subject because you are true?

Venus heard me sigh this song,
And by love's sweetest part, variety, she swore 20
She heard not this till now, and that it should be so no
          more.
She went, examined, and returned ere long,
    And said, "Alas, some two or three
    Poor heretics in love there be,
    Which think to 'stablish dangerous constancy, 25
But I have told them, 'Since you will be true,
You shall be true to them who are false to you.'"

Confined Love

Some man unworthy to be possessor
Of old or new love, himself being false or weak,
  Thought his pain and shame would be lesser
If on womankind he might his anger wreak;
    And thence a law did grow: 5
    One might but one man know.
    But are other creatures so?

Are sun, moon, or stars by law forbidden
To smile where they list, or lend away their light?

11 do as did your mothers *i.e.*, be promiscuous 17 **travail**
(1) suffering, (2) travel **thorough** through 26 **will be in-
sist** on being

10   Are birds divorced, or are they chidden
     If they leave their mate, or lie abroad a night?
             Beasts do no jointures lose
             Though they new lovers choose,
             But we are made worse than those.

15   Who e'er rigged fair ship to lie in harbors,
     And not to seek new lands, or not to deal withal?
             Or built fair houses, set trees and arbors,
     Only to lock up, or else to let them fall?
             Good is not good unless
20   A thousand it possess,
             But doth waste with greediness.

Love's Diet

     To what a cumbersome unwieldiness
     And burdenous corpulence my love had grown
             But that I did, to make it less
             And keep it in proportión,
5   Give it a diet, made it feed upon
     That which love worst endures, discretión.

     Above one sigh a day I allowed him not,
     Of which my fortune and my faults had part;
             And if sometimes by stealth he got
10   A she sigh from my mistress' heart
     And thought to feast on that, I let him see
     'Twas neither very sound, nor meant to me.

     If he wrung from me a tear, I brined it so
     With scorn or shame that him it nourished not;
15   If he sucked hers, I let him know
             'Twas not a tear which he had got;
     His drink was counterfeit as was his meat;
     For eyes which roll towards all weep not, but sweat.

11 a night at night   16 deal withal trade with   2 had would
have   3 But that I did if I did not   8 fortune bad fortune
12 sound i.e., sincere to for   17 meat i.e., his allowance of
sighs

Whatever he would dictate, I writ that,
But burnt my letters. When she writ to me,   20
    And that that favor made him fat,
    I said, if any title be
Conveyed by this, ah, what doth it avail
To be the fortieth name in an entail?

Thus I reclaimed my buzzard love to fly   25
At what, and when, and how, and where I choose;
    Now negligent of sport I lie,
    And now as other falc'ners use,
I spring a mistress, swear, write, sigh, and weep;
And the game killed or lost, go talk, and sleep.   30

Love's Deity

I long to talk with some old lover's ghost
    Who died before the god of love was born.
I cannot think that he who then loved most
    Sunk so low as to love one which did scorn.
But since this god produced a destiny,   5
And that vice-nature, custom, lets it be,
    I must love her that loves not me.

Sure they which made him god meant not so much,
    Nor he in his young godhead practised it.
But when an even flame two hearts did touch,   10
    His office was indulgently to fit
Actives to passives. Correspondency
Only, his subject was. It cannot be
    Love till I love her that loves me.

But every modern god will now extend   15
    His vast prerogative as far as Jove.

21 **that that** when that   24 **entail** the settlement of the future
ownership of a landed estate, naming those who are to inherit
it if the direct line of descent fails to provide an heir   25 **re-
claimed** called back   **buzzard** inferior hawk   28 **use** are in the
habit of doing   29 **spring** flush (a bird) from cover   5 **pro-
duced a destiny** instituted a (hard) fate for lovers   6 **vice-
nature** other nature   8 **meant not so much** had no idea of
giving him so much power   10 **even** equal (in intensity)   15
modern ordinary   **will** wishes to

To rage, to lust, to write to, to commend,
　　　All is the purlieu of the god of love.
Oh were we wakened by this tyranny
20　To ungod this child again, it could not be
　　　　　I should love her who loves not me.

Rebel and atheist too, why murmur I
　　　As though I felt the worst that Love could do?
Love might make me leave loving, or might try
25　　A deeper plague, to make her love me too,
　　Which, since she loves before, I am loath to see.
　Falsehood is worse than hate, and that must be
　　　　If she whom I love should love me.

Love's Exchange

　Love, any devil else but you
Would for a given soul give something too.
　　At court your fellows every day
Give the art of rhyming, huntsmanship, or play
5　　For them which were their own before.
　　Only I have nothing, which gave more,
But am, alas, by being lowly, lower.

　I ask no dispensation now
To falsify a tear or sigh or vow;
10　　I do not sue from thee to draw
A *non obstante* on nature's law.
　　These are prerogatives; they inhere
　　In thee and thine; none should forswear
Except that he Love's minion were.

15　　Give me thy weakness, make me blind
Both ways, as thou and thine, in eyes and mind;
　　Love, let me never know that this
Is love, or that love childish is.
　　Let me not know that others know

18 **purlieu** province　27 **falsehood** *i.e.*, deserting whom she loved before　4 **play** gambling　6 **have** have received　11 *non obstante* **on** exception from　12 **perogatives** inherent rights

That she knows my pains, lest that so   20
A tender shame make me mine own new woe.

If thou give nothing, yet thou art just,
Because I would not thy first motions trust;
   Small towns which stand stiff till great shot
Enforce them, by war's law condition not.   25
   Such in love's warfare is my case:
   I may not article for grace,
Having put Love at last to show this face—

This face, by which he could command
And change the idolatry of any land,   30
   This face, which wheresoe'er it comes,
Can call vowed men from cloisters, dead from tombs,
   And melt both poles at once, and store
   Deserts with cities, and make more
Mines in the earth than quarries were before.   35

For this, Love is enraged with me;
Yet kills not. If I must example be
   To future rebels, if the unborn
Must learn by my being cut up and torn,
   Kill and dissect me, Love; for this   40
   Torture against thine own end is:
Racked carcasses make ill anatomies.

Farewell to Love

   Whilst yet to prove,
I thought there was some deity in love;
   So did I reverence and gave
Worship. As atheists at their dying hour
Call what they cannot name an unknown power,   5
   As ignorantly did I crave.
       Thus when

23 **motions** promptings 24 **stand stiff** hold out (against a
siege) 25 **condition** make conditions (of surrender) 27
article stipulate, negotiate 28 **this face** *i.e.*, this woman's face
42 **Racked** tortured, stretched on the rack **anatomies** corpses
for dissection 1 **prove** know by experience

Things not yet known are coveted by men,
Our desires give them fashión, and so
10 As they wax lesser, fall, as they size, grow.

But, from late fair
His highness sitting in a golden chair
Is not less cared for after three days
By children, than the thing which lovers so
15 Blindly admire and with such worship woo;
Being had, enjoying it decays;
And thence
What before pleased them all takes but one sense,
And that so lamely as it leaves behind
20 A kind of sorrowing dullness to the mind.

Ah cannot we,
As well as cocks and lions, jocund be
After such pleasures? Unless wise
Nature decreed (since each such act, they say,
25 Diminisheth the length of life a day)
This, as she would man should despise
The sport
Because that other curse of being short
And only for a minute made to be
30 Eagers desires to raise posterity.

Since so, my mind
Shall not desire what no man else can find,
I'll no more dote and run
To pursue things which had endamaged me;
35 And when I come where moving beauties be,
As men do when the summer's sun
Grows great,
Though I admire their greatness, shun their heat;
Each place can afford shadows. If all fail,
40 'Tis but applying wormseed to the tail.

9 fashion form   10 fall *i.e.*, our desires wane   size increase
12 His highness toy king   16 decays impairs (the object is
it)   18 all *i.e.*, all the senses   takes pleases, captivates   19 as
that   40 'Tis but it's only a matter of   wormseed plant which
expels intestinal worms (and allays sexual desire)

The Flea

Mark but this flea, and mark in this
How little that which thou deny'st me is;
  It sucked me first, and now sucks thee,
And in this flea our two bloods mingled be.
  Thou know'st that this cannot be said   5
A sin, nor shame, nor loss of maidenhead;
  Yet this enjoys before it woo,
And pampered, swells with one blood made of two,
And this, alas, is more than we would do.

O stay, three lives in one flea spare,   10
Where we almost, yea more than married are.
  This flea is you and I, and this
Our marriage bed and marriage temple is;
  Though parents grudge, and you, we're met
And cloistered in these living walls of jet.   15
  Though use make you apt to kill me,
Let not to that, self-murder added be,
And sacrilege: three sins in killing three.

Cruel and sudden, hast thou since
Purpled thy nail in blood of innocence?   20
  Wherein could this flea guilty be,
Except in that drop which it sucked from thee?
  Yet thou triumph'st, and say'st that thou
Find'st not thyself nor me the weaker now.
  'Tis true. Then learn how false fears be: 25
Just so much honor, when thou yield'st to me,
Will waste, as this flea's death took life from thee.

The Will

Before I sigh my last gasp, let me breathe,
Great Love, some legacies: Here I bequeath
Mine eyes to Argus, if mine eyes can see;

4 **bloods mingled be** as sperm in the womb   16 **use** custom,
habit   18 **sacrilege** *i.e.*, the destruction of the temple (1. 13)
3 **Argus** the watchman who had a hundred eyes

If they be blind, then, Love, I give them thee;
5   My tongue to Fame, to ambassadors mine ears,
      To women or the sea my tears.
    Thou, Love, hast taught me heretofore,
By making me serve her who had twenty more,
That I should give to none but such as had too much be-
      fore.

10   My constancy I to the planets give,
My truth to them who at the court do live,
Mine ingenuity and openness
To Jesuits, to buffoons my pensiveness,
My silence to any who abroad hath been,
15   My money to a Capuchin.
    Thou Love, taught'st me, by appointing me
To love there where no love received can be,
Only to give to such as have an incapacity.

My faith I give to Roman Catholics,
20   All my good works unto the schísmatics
Of Amsterdam, my best civility
And courtship to an university;
My modesty I give to soldiers bare;
      My patiénce let gamesters share.
25   Thou, Love, taught'st me, by making me
Love her that holds my love disparity,
Only to give to those that count my gifts indignity.

I give my reputatión to those
Which were my friends, mine industry to foes;
30   To schoolmen I bequeath my doubtfulness,
My sickness to physicians or excess,

---

12 **ingenuity** ingenuousness 13 **buffoons** clowns (who talk
much and think little) 15 **Capuchin** whose habit is made
without pockets 19 **faith** (justification by faith is a Protestant
doctrine) 20 **good works** (emphasized by the Roman Catho-
lics more than by the Protestants, especially such extremists as
the schismatics of Amsterdam) 21 **civility** politeness 22
courtship courtiership 26 **disparity** *i.e.*, of insufficient value
30 **schoolmen** philosophers of the (medieval) universities, fa-
mous for exquisite distinctions 31 **excess** intemperance (cause
of sickness)

To nature all that I in rhyme have writ,
  And to my company my wit.
  Thou, Love, by making me adore
Her who begot this love in me before,   35
Taught'st me to make as though I gave when I did but
  restore.

To him for whom the passing-bell next tolls
I give my physic books; my written rolls
Of moral counsels I to Bedlam give,
My brazen medals unto them which live   40
In want of bread, to them which pass among
  All foreigners, mine English tongue.
  Thou, Love, by making me love one
Who thinks her friendship a fit portión
For younger lovers, dost my gifts thus disproportión. 45

Therefore I'll give no more; but I'll undo
The world by dying, because love dies too.
Then all your beauties will be no more worth
Than gold in mines where none doth draw it forth,
And all your graces no more use shall have   50
  Than a sundial in a grave.
  Thou, Love, taught'st me, by making me
Love her who doth neglect both me and thee,
To invent and practice this one way to annihilate all three.

The Damp

When I am dead, and doctors know not why,
  And my friends' curiosity
Will have me cut up to survey each part,
When they shall find your picture in my heart,
  You think a sudden damp of love   5
  Will through all their senses move,
And work on them as me, and so prefer
Your murder to the name of massacre.

33 **company** associates, friends 37 **passing-bell** bell rung for
a dying man 38 **physic** medical 39 **Bedlam** the London
madhouse 5 **damp** vapor 7 **prefer** advance, raise

Poor victories! But if you dare be brave,
10   And pleasure in your conquest have,
First kill the enormous giant, your disdain,
And let the enchantress honor next be slain,
   And like a Goth and Vandal rise,
   Deface recórds and histories
15 Of your own arts and triumphs over men,
And without such advantage kill me then.

For I could muster up, as well as you,
   My giants, and my witches too,
Which are vast constancy and secretness,
20 But these I neither look for nor profess.
   Kill me as woman; let me die
   As a mere man; do you but try
Your passive valor, and you shall find than,
Naked, you've odds enough of any man.

The Triple Fool

   I am two fools, I know,
  For loving, and for saying so
   In whining poetry.
(But where's that wise man that would not be I
5   If she would not deny?)
Then as the earth's inward, narrow, crooked lanes
Do purge sea water's fretful salt away,
  I thought if I could draw my pains
Through rhyme's vexation, I should them allay.
1٠ Grief brought to numbers cannot be so fierce,
For he tames it that fetters it in verse.

   But when I have done so,
  Some man, his art and voice to show,
   Doth set and sing my pain,
15 And by delighting many, frees again
   Grief, which verse did restrain.
To love and grief tribute of verse belongs,

20 profess impute to myself 23 than then 24 Naked unaided
10 numbers verse

But not of such as pleases when 'tis read;
  Both are increasèd by such songs,
For both their triumphs so are publishèd,   20
And I, which was two fools, do so grow three.
Who are a little wise, the best fools be.

The Blossom

  Little think'st thou, poor flower,
    Whom I have watched six or seven days,
And seen thy birth, and seen what every hour
Gave to thy growth, thee to this height to raise,
And now dost laugh and triumph on this bough;   5
      Little think'st thou
That it will freeze anon, and that I shall
Tomorrow find thee fall'n, or not at all.

  Little think'st thou, poor heart,
    That labor'st yet to nestle thee,   10
And think'st by hovering here to get a part
In a forbidden or forbidding tree,
And hop'st her stiffness by long siege to bow;
      Little think'st thou
That thou tomorrow, ere that sun doth wake,   15
Must with this sun and me a journey take.

  But thou, which lov'st to be
    Subtle to plague thyself, wilt say,
"Alas, if you must go, what's that to me?
Here lies my business, and here I will stay.   20
You go to friends whose love and means present
      Various content
To your eyes, ears, and tongue, and every part.
If then your body go, what need you a heart?"

  Well then, stay here; but know,   25
    When thou hast stayed and done thy most,
A naked, thinking heart that makes no show

21 grow become   10 nestle thee settle yourself (as a squatter)
15 that sun *i.e.,* the lady

Is to a woman but a kind of ghost.
How shall she know my heart, or having none,
30   Know thee for one?
Practice may make her know some other part,
But take my word, she doth not know a heart.

  Meet me at London, then,
 Twenty days hence, and thou shalt see
35 Me fresher and more fat by being with men
Than if I had stayed still with her and thee.
For God's sake, if you can, be you so too.
  I would give you
There to another friend, whom we shall find
40 As glad to have my body as my mind.

Negative Love

 I never stooped so low as they
 Which on an eye, cheek, lip can prey;
  Seldom to them which soar no higher
  Than virtue or the mind to admire,
5 For sense and understanding may
  Know what gives fuel to their fire.
 My love, though silly, is more brave,
 For may I miss whene'er I crave,
 If I know yet what I would have.

10 If that be simply perfectest
 Which can by no way be expressed
  But negatives, my love is so.
  To all which all love, I say no.
 If any who deciphers best
15   What we know not, ourselves, can know,
 Let him teach me that nothing. This
 As yet my ease and comfort is:
 Though I speed not, I cannot miss.

3 **to them** as low as those 7 **silly** innocent **brave** admirable
8 **miss** fail, lose out **crave** *i.e.*, a woman 15 **ourselves** (alludes to the maxim "know thyself") 18 **speed** succeed

The Broken Heart

He is stark mad, whoever says
That he hath been in love an hour,
    Yet not that love so soon decays,
But that it can ten in less space devour.
        Who will believe me if I swear   5
        That I have had the plague a year?
Who would not laugh at me if I should say
I saw a flask of powder burn a day?

    Ah, what a trifle is a heart
If once into Love's hands it come!   10
    All other griefs allow a part
To other griefs, and ask themselves but some;
        They come to us, but us Love draws;
        He swallows us and never chaws;
By him, as by chained shot, whole ranks do die;   15
He is the tyrant pike, our hearts the fry.

    If 'twere not so, what did become
Of my heart when I first saw thee?
    I brought a heart into the room,
But from the room I carried none with me.   20
        If it had gone to thee, I know
        Mine would have taught thine heart to show
More pity unto me; but Love, alas,
At one first blow did shiver it as glass.

    Yet nothing can to nothing fall,   25
Nor any place be empty quite;
    Therefore I think my breast hath all
Those pieces still, though they be not unite;
        And now as broken glasses show
        A hundred lesser faces, so   30
My rags of heart can like, wish, and adore,
But after one such love can love no more.

15 **chained shot** balls chained together discharged from a cannon   16 **tyrant** voracious   **fry** the small fish (which the pike preys on)   25 **Yet . . . fall** *i.e.*, matter is indestructible   31 **rags** remnants

The Prohibition

Take heed of loving me;
At least remember I forbade it thee;
    Not that I shall repair my unthrifty waste
Of breath and blood upon thy sighs and tears,
5   By being to thee then what to me thou wast;
But so great joy our life at once outwears.
    Then, lest thy love by my death frustrate be,
    If thou love me, take heed of loving me.

        Take heed of hating me,
10   Or too much triumph in the victory;
    Not that I shall be mine own officer,
And hate with hate again retaliate,
    But thou wilt lose the style of conqueror
If I, thy conquest, perish by thy hate.
15   Then, lest my being nothing lessen thee,
    If thou hate me, take heed of hating me.

        Yet love and hate me too,
So these extremes shall neither's office do;
    Love me, that I may die the gentler way;
20   Hate me, because thy love is too great for me;
    Or let these two themselves, not me, decay;
So shall I live thy stage, not triumph be.
    Then, lest thy love, hate, and me thou undo,
    Oh let me live; yet love and hate me too.

The Primrose

Upon this primrose hill,
Where if heav'n would distill
A shower of rain, each several drop might go
To his own primrose, and grow manna so,

3 **repair** make good 4 **upon** by drawing upon 11 **officer**
executor of justice 12 **again** in return 13 **style** title 18
neither's office *i.e.*, killing him with joy (l. 6) or destroying
him (l. 14) 21 **decay** waste, destroy 22 **stage** (for the re-
peated exhibition of your powers) **triumph** *i.e.*, victim 23
undo destroy 3 **several** separate 4 **grow** become

And where their form and their infinity   5
   Make a terrestrial galaxy
   As the small stars do in the sky,
I walk to find a true-love; and I see
That 'tis not a mere woman that is she,
But must or more or less than woman be.   10

   Yet know I not which flower
   I wish, a six or four,
For should my true love less than woman be,
She were scarce anything; and then, should she
Be more than woman, she would get above   15
   All thought of sex and think to move
   My heart to study her, and not to love.
Both these were monsters. Since there must reside
Falsehood in woman, I could more abide
She were by art than nature falsified.   20

   Live, primrose, then, and thrive
   With thy true number, five;
And women, whom this flower doth represent,
With this mysterious number be content.
Ten is the farthest number; if half ten   25
   Belong unto each woman, then
   Each woman may take half us men;
Or if this will not serve their turn, since all
Numbers are odd or even, and they fall
First into this five, women may take us all.   30

Air and Angels

Twice or thrice had I loved thee
   Before I knew thy face or name
   (So in a voice, so in a shapeless flame
Angels affect us oft, and worshipped be);

8 true-love abnormal primrose with four or six petals   **10 or more** either more   **18 were** would be   **monsters** unnatural creatures   **25 farthest number** highest (simple, uncompounded) number   **29 they** *i.e.*, an odd number (3) and an even number (2)   **1 loved thee** *i.e.*, loved other women seeking what I subsequently found in you   **4 affect** visit, haunt

5   Still when to where thou wert I came,
Some lovely glorious nothing I did see.
         But since my soul, whose child love is,
Takes limbs of flesh (and else could nothing do),
         More subtle than the parent is
10   Love must not be, but take a body too;
And therefore what thou wert, and who,
         I bid love ask, and now
That it assume thy body I allow,
And fix itself in thy lip, eye, and brow.

15   Whilst thus to ballast love I thought
         (And so more steadily to have gone),
         With wares which would sink admiratión
I saw I had love's pinnace overfraught.
         Ev'ry thy hair for love to work upon
20   Is much too much; some fitter must be sought.
         For nor in nothing, nor in things
Extreme and scattering bright can love inhere.
         Then, as an angel, face and wings
Of air not pure as it, yet pure, doth wear,
25   So thy love may be my love's sphere.
              Just such disparity
As is 'twixt air and angels' purity,
'Twixt women's love and men's will ever be.

Lovers' Infiniteness

If yet I have not all thy love,
    Dear, I shall never have it all;
I cannot breathe one other sigh to move,
    Nor can entreat one other tear to fall,
5 And all my treasure which should purchase thee,

5 **Still** always   6 **some lovely glorious nothing** *i.e.*, something
angelic   17 **sink** overwhelm   18 **overfraught** overloaded   20
some fitter *i.e.*, some fitter embodiment for love   22 **scattering**
dazzling   24 **wear** (to appear to men, angels take a body of air,
less pure than the angel's own essence)   25 **sphere** the orbit of
a heavenly body, controlled by an angel or intelligence (**my
love**)

Sighs, tears, and oaths, and letters I have spent.
Yet no more can be due to me
   Than at the bargain made was meant.
If then thy gift of love were partiál,
That some to me, some should to others fall,   10
Dear, I shall never have thee all.

Or if then thou gavest me all,
   All was but all which thou hadst then;
But if in thy heart since there be, or shall
   New love created be by other men   15
Which have their stocks entire, and can in tears,
   In sighs, in oaths, and letters outbid me,
This new love may beget new fears,
   For this love was not vowed by thee.
And yet it was: thy gift being general,   20
The ground, thy heart, is mine; whatever shall
Grow there, dear, I should have it all.

Yet I would not have all yet.
   He that hath all can have no more,
And since my love doth every day admit   25
   New growth, thou shouldst have new rewards in store.
Thou canst not every day give me thy heart;
   If thou canst give it, then thou never gavest it.
Love's riddles are that though thy heart depart,
   It stays at home, and thou with losing savest it.   30
But we will have a way more liberal
Than changing hearts—to join them, so we shall
Be one, and one another's all.

Witchcraft by a Picture

   I fix mine eye on thine, and there
      Pity my picture burning in thine eye;
   My picture drowned in a transparent tear,
      When I look lower I espy.
         Hadst thou the wicked skill   5

16 **stocks** *i.e.*, of treasure (ll. 5-6)

By pictures made and marred to kill,
How many ways mightst thou perform thy will!

But now I've drunk thy sweet salt tears,
   And though thou pour more, I'll depart;
10 My picture vanished, vanish fears
   That I can be endamaged by that art.
     Though thou retain of me
One picture more, yet that will be,
Being in thine own heart, from all malice free.

Break of Day

'Tis true, 'tis day. What though it be?
Oh, wilt thou therefore rise from me?
   Why should we rise because 'tis light?
   Did we lie down because 'twas night?
5 Love, which in spite of darkness brought us hether,
Should in despite of light keep us together.

Light hath no tongue, but is all eye;
If it could speak as well as spy,
   This were the worst that it could say:
10   That being well I fain would stay,
And that I loved my heart and honor so
That I would not from him that had them go.

Must business thee from hence remove?
Oh, that's the worst disease of love;
   The poor, the foul, the false, love can
15   Admit, but not the busied man.
He which hath business and makes love doth do
Such wrong as when a married man doth woo.

6 **pictures** (witches were reputed to kill by making and destroy-
ing images of their victims) 11 **art** witchcraft **Break of Day**
spoken by a woman 5 **hether** hither 10 **fain** gladly 15 **foul**
ugly

A Valediction: of my Name
in the Window

My name engraved herein
Doth cóntribute my firmness to this glass,
    Which, ever since that charm, hath been
    As hard as that which graved it was.
Thine eye will give it price enough to mock   5
    The diamonds of either rock.

'Tis much that glass should be
As all-confessing and through-shine as I;
    'Tis more that it shows thee to thee,
    And clear reflects thee to thine eye.   10
But all such rules, love's magic can undo:
    Here you see me, and I am you.

As no one point nor dash,
Which are but áccessóries to this name,
    The showers and tempests can outwash,   15
    So shall all times find me the same;
You this entireness better may fulfill,
    Who have the pattern with you still.

Or if too hard and deep
This learning be for a scratched name to teach,   20
    It as a given death's head keep,
    Lovers' mortality to preach,
Or think this ragged bony name to be
    My ruinous anatomy.

Then, as all my souls be   25
Emparadised in you (in whom alone

1 **herein** *i.e.,* in this glass   3 **charm** *i.e.,* the name or the writing
of it   5 **price** value   **mock** set at nought   6 **of either rock** from
old or new mines   8 **through-shine** transparent   12 **me** literally,
my name   **I am you** *i.e.,* lovers are one   13 **point** mark of punc-
tuation   17 **entireness** sincerity   **fulfill** follow   21 **death's head**
skull kept in view as a reminder of human mortality   25 **all
my souls** *i.e.,* the three functions of the soul—growth, sensa-
tion (**see**), reason (**understand**)

I understand, and grow, and see),
The rafters of my body, bone,
Being still with you, the muscle, sinew, and vein
30   Which tile this house will come again.

Till my return, repair
And recompact my scattered body so.
As all the virtuous powers which are
Fixed in the stars are said to flow
35   Into such characters as gravèd be
When these stars have supremacy,

So since this name was cut
When love and grief their exaltation had,
No door 'gainst this name's influence shut;
40   As much more loving as more sad
'Twill make thee, and thou shouldst, till I return,
Since I die daily, daily mourn.

When thy inconsiderate hand
Flings ope this casement with my trembling name,
45   To look on one whose wit or land
New batt'ry to thy heart may frame,
Then think this name alive, and that thou thus
In it offend'st my genius.

And when thy melted maid,
50   Corrupted by thy lover's gold—and page,
His letter at thy pillow hath laid,
Disputed it, and tamed thy rage,
And thou beginn'st to thaw towards him for this,
May my name step in and hide his.

55   And if this treason go
To an overt act, and that thou write again;

28 **bone** skeleton, *i.e.*, the name scratched on the window   33 **virtuous powers** power of influencing human affairs   35 **characters** *i.e.*, those of the astrologer's horoscope   38 **exaltation** eminence, greatest influence (an astrological term)   41 **'Twill** *i.e.*, not shutting the door will   43 **inconsiderate** thoughtless 48 **genius** guardian spirit   49 **melted** softened, worked on   52 **Disputed** discussed   56 **that** if   **again** in reply

In superscribing, this name flow
Into thy fancy from the pane.
So, in forgetting thou rememb'rest right,
    And unaware to me shalt write.   60

But glass and lines must be
No means our firm, substantial love to keep;
    Near death inflicts this lethargy,
    And this I murmur in my sleep.
Impute this idle talk to that I go, .   65
    For dying men talk often so.

Song

Sweetest love, I do not go
    For weariness of thee,
Nor in hope the world can show
    A fitter love for me;
        But since that I   5
Must die at last, 'tis best
To use myself in jest
    Thus by feigned deaths to die.

Yesternight the sun went hence,
    And yet is here today;   10
He hath no desire nor sense,
    Nor half so short a way.
        Then fear not me,
But believe that I shall make
Speedier journeys, since I take   15
    More wings and spurs than he.

O how feeble is man's power,
    That if good fortune fall,
Cannot add another hour,

---

57 superscribing addressing (the letter) **flow** may . . . flow
62 firm not brittle, like glass   **substantial** not one-dimensional,
like a line   **65 that I go** the fact that I go   **66 dying** *i.e.,* part-
ing   **7 use** accustom   **jest** sport, play   **8 feigned deaths** *i.e.,*
absences

20   Nor a lost hour recall!
          But come bad chance,
       And we join to it our strength,
       And we teach it art and length,
          Itself o'er us to advance.

25   When thou sigh'st, thou sigh'st not wind,
          But sigh'st my soul away;
       When thou weep'st, unkindly kind,
          My life's blood doth decay.
             It cannot be
30   That thou lov'st me as thou say'st,
       If in thine my life thou waste.
          Thou art the best of me.

       Let not thy divining heart
          Forethink me any ill;
35   Destiny may take thy part,
          And may thy fears fulfill;
             But think that we
       Are but turned aside to sleep.
       They who one another keep
40   Alive, ne'er parted be.

A Valediction: of the Book

       I'll tell thee now, dear love, what thou shalt do
          To anger destiny as she doth us,
       How I shall stay though she esloign me thus,
       And how posterity shall know it too,
5   How thine may out-endure
             Sibyl's glory, and obscure
             Her who from Pindar could allure,

26 **sigh'st my soul away** (because every sigh costs a drop of
blood) 27 **unkindly** unnaturally (because it is not the nature of
women to be sympathetic) 28 **blood doth decay** (because
sorrow dries the blood) title **book** collection of written records,
i.e., letters 3 **esloign** carry off 6 **Sibyl's** of an ancient
prophetess, here a type of long duration 7 **Her** Corinna, a
lyric poetess who is said to have defeated Pindar five times
in competition

And her through whose help Lucan is not lame,
And her whose book, they say, Homer did find and name.

Study our manuscripts, those myriads 10
    Of letters which have passed 'twixt thee and me;
    Thence write our annals, and in them will be
To all whom love's subliming fire invades,
      Rule and example found;
        There, the faith of any ground 15
      No schismatic will dare to wound,
That sees how Love this grace to us affords,
To make, to keep, to use, to be these his records.

This book as long-lived as the elements
    Or as the world's form, this all-gravèd tome 20
    In cipher writ or new made idiom
(We for Love's clergy only are instruments),
      When this book is made thus,
        Should again the ravenous
      Vandals and Goths inundate us, 25
Learning were safe; in this our universe
Schools might learn sciences, spheres music, angels verse.

Here Love's divines, since all divinity
    Is love or wonder, may find all they seek,
    Whether abstract spiritual love they like, 30
Their souls exhaled with what they do not see,
      Or loath so to amuse
        Faith's infirmity, they choose
      Something which they may see and use;
For though mind be the heaven where love doth sit, 35
Beauty a convenient type may be to figure it.

8 her his wife, who assisted him in the composition of the
Pharsalia 9 her Phantasia, a woman of Memphis, the reputed
author of a poem on the Trojan war and another on the return
of Ulysses to Ithaca upon which Homer is said to have drawn
heavily name give his name to 13 subliming purifying 15
the faith of any ground belief in any fundamental principle
20 the world's form the creation 22 We *i.e.*, in our letters
(this book) instruments service books 25 inundate overrun
27 music *i.e.*, that supposed to be made by the revolution of
the heavenly spheres 31 exhaled drawn out 32 amuse puzzle
36 figure picture, represent

Here more than in their books may lawyers find
  Both by what titles mistresses are ours
  And how prerogative these states devours,
40 Transferred from Love himself to womankind,
   Who, though from heart and eyes
   They exact great subsidies,
  Forsake him who on them relies,
  And for the cause, honor or conscience give—
45 Chimeras vain as they or their prerogative.

Here statesmen, or of them they which can read,
  May of their occupation find the grounds.
  Love and their art alike it deadly wounds
If to consider what 'tis, one proceed.
50   In both they do excel
   Who the present govern well,
  Whose weakness none doth or dares tell.
In this thy book, such will their nothing see,
As in the Bible some can find out alchemy.

55 Thus vent thy thoughts. Abroad I'll study thee,
  As he removes far off that great heights takes:
  How great love is, presence best trial makes,
But absence tries how long this love will be;
   To take a latitude
60   Sun or stars are fitliest viewed
  At their brightest, but to conclude
Of longitudes, what other way have we
But to mark when and where the dark eclipses be?

39 **prerogative** privilege, *i.e.*, the arbitrary behavior of women
states estates (held by **titles**)   42 **subsidies** contributions of
money   43 **relies** *i.e.*, expects some return   44 **give** allege
(honor or conscience to be the reason for holding out on the
lover)   45 **chimeras** wild fancies **vain** worthless   53 **their
nothing** the grounds of their occupation, which is nothing   55
vent utter   56 **takes** measures   57 **trial** test   61 **at their
brightest** *i.e.*, at their zenith   62 **longitudes** *i.e.*, the duration
of love

A Valediction: of Weeping

Let me pour forth
My tears before thy face whilst I stay here,
For thy face coins them, and thy stamp they bear,
And by this mintage they are something worth,
    For thus they be   5
    Pregnant of thee;
Fruits of much grief they are, emblems of more:
When a tear falls, that thou falls which it bore;
So thou and I are nothing then, when on a divers shore.

    On a round ball   10
A workman that hath copies by can lay
An Europe, Afric, and an Asia,
And quickly make that which was nothing, all;
    So doth each tear
    Which thee doth wear,   15
A globe, yea world, by that impression grow,
Till thy tears mixed with mine do overflow
This world: by waters sent from thee, my heaven dis-
    solvèd so.

    O more than moon,
Draw not up seas to drown me in thy sphere,   20
Weep me not dead in thine arms, but forbear
To teach the sea what it may do too soon;
    Let not the wind
    Example find
To do me more harm than it purposeth;   25
Since thou and I sigh one another's breath,
Whoe'er sighs most is cruelest, and hastes the other's
    death.

2 **whilst I stay here** (implies imminent separation) 6 **Pregnant of** replete with 7 **grief** *i.e.*, that of parting **more** *i.e.*, the grief of separation 8 **that thou . . . which it bore** that you whose stamp it bears 15 **thee** *i.e.*, your stamp 16 **impression** stamp **grow** turn into 18 **by . . . so** as if the waters above the firmament should inundate the heavens 22 **do** *i.e.*, drown me 27 **death** *i.e.*, by sighing, which wastes the blood and hastens death

A Valediction: Forbidding Mourning

As virtuous men pass mildly away,
   And whisper to their souls to go,
Whilst some of their sad friends do say,
   "The breath goes now," and some say, "No,"

5 So let us melt and make no noise,
   No tear-floods nor sigh-tempests move;
'Twere profanation of our joys
   To tell the laity our love.

Moving of the earth brings harms and fears;
10   Men reckon what it did and meant;
But trepidation of the spheres,
   Though greater far, is innocent.

Dull sublunary lovers' love,
   Whose soul is sense, cannot admit
15 Absence. because it doth remove
   Those things which elemented it.

But we by a love so much refined
   That ourselves know not what it is,
Interassurèd of the mind,
20   Care less eyes, lips, and hands to miss.

Our two souls, therefore, which are one,
   Though I must go, endure not yet
A breach, but an expansión,
   Like gold to airy thinness beat.

25 If they be two, they are two so
   As stiff twin compasses are two;
Thy soul, the fixed foot, makes no show
   To move, but doth if the other do.

9 **Moving of the earth** an earthquake 11 **trepidation** the oscillation imputed to the eighth (or ninth) sphere of the Ptolemaic astronomy (a cosmic, as opposed to a terrestrial, phenomenon) 12 **innocent** harmless 13 **sublunary** earthly 14 **admit** endure 16 **elemented** composed 24 **airy thinness** i.e., that of gold leaf

And though it in the center sit,
   Yet when the other far doth roam,   30
It leans and hearkens after it,
   And grows erect as that comes home.

Such wilt thou be to me, who must,
   Like the other foot, obliquely run;
Thy firmness makes my circle just,   35
   And makes me end where I begun.

The Expiration

So, so, break off this last lamenting kiss,
   Which sucks two souls, and vapors both away;
Turn thou, ghost, that way, and let me turn this,
   And let ourselves benight our happiest day;
We asked none leave to love, nor will we owe   5
Any so cheap a death as saying "Go."

"Go!" And if that word have not quite killed thee,
   Ease me with death by bidding me go too.
Oh, if it have, let my word work on me,
   And a just office on a murderer do,   10
Except it be too late to kill me so,
Being double dead, going, and bidding go

The Ecstasy

Where, like a pillow on a bed,
   A pregnant bank swelled up to rest
The violet's reclining head,
   Sat we two, one another's best.

34 **obliquely** in a circle 35 **just** complete, perfect **The Expiration** entitled *Valediction* in some manuscripts 2 **vapors** . . . **away** causes to pass away as vapor 4 **benight** overcloud, darken **The Ecstasy** an experience, attained by intense concentration and self-purification, in which the soul quits the body to contemplate the divine at close range

Our hands were firmly cémented
    With a fast balm which thence did spring,
Our eye-beams twisted, and did thread
    Our eyes upon one double string;

So to intergraft our hands, as yet
10   Was all the means to make us one,
And pictures on our eyes to get
    Was all our propagatión.

As 'twixt two equal armies fate
    Suspends uncertain victory,
15 Our souls, which to advance their state
    Were gone out, hung 'twixt her and me.

And whilst our souls negotiate there,
    We like sepulchral statues lay;
All day the same our postures were,
20   And we said nothing all the day.

If any so by love refined
    That he soul's language understood,
And by good love were grown all mind,
    Within convenient distance stood,

25 He (though he knew not which soul spake,
    Because both meant, both spake the same)
Might thence a new concoction take,
    And part far purer than he came.

This ecstasy doth unperplex,
30   We said, and tell us what we love;
We see by this it was not sex,
    We see we saw not what did move;

6 **fast balm** adhesive oily substance (presumably that thought
to inhere in and preserve all bodies)   7 **eye-beams** invisible
rays emitted by the eyes which carry images to the brain, *i.e.*,
our looks were intent on each other   11 **get** beget   27 **concoction** state of perfection   32 **move** *i.e.*, move us to love, *viz.*,
spiritual affinity

But as all several souls contain
    Mixture of things, they know not what,
Love these mixed souls doth mix again   35
    And makes both one, each this and that.

A single violet transplant,
    The strength, the color, and the size
(All which before was poor and scant)
    Redoubles still and multiplies.   40

When love with one another so
    Interinanimates two souls,
That abler soul which thence doth flow
    Defects of loneliness controls.

We then, who are this new soul, know   45
    Of what we are composed and made,
For the atomies of which we grow
    Are souls, whom no change can invade.

But oh, alas, so long, so far
    Our bodies why do we forbear?   50
They're ours, though they're not we; we are
    The intelligences, they the spheres;

We owe them thanks because they thus
    Did us to us at first convey,
Yielded their forces, sense, to us,   55
    Nor are dross to us, but allay.

On man heaven's influence works not so,
    But that it first imprints the air;
So soul into the soul may flow
    Though it to body first repair.   60

33 several separate and distinct   **44 controls** overcomes   **47 atomies** atoms   **50 forbear** abstain from using   **52 intelligences** angels who guide the heavenly bodies (spheres)   **55 sense** sensations   **56 allay** alloy   **57 influence** the ethereal fluid by which the stars exercise their control over human destiny

As our blood labors to beget
    Spirits as like souls as it can,
Because such fingers need to knit
    That subtle knot which makes us man,

65   So must pure lovers' souls descend
       To affections and to faculties
Which sense may reach and apprehend
    Else a great prince in prison lies.

To our bodies turn we then, that so
70   Weak men on love revealed may look;
Love's mysteries in souls do grow,
    But yet the body is his book.

And if some lover, such as we,
    Have heard this dialogue of one,
75   Let him still mark us, he shall see
      Small change when we are to bodies gone.

A Fever

Oh do not die, for I shall hate
    All women so when thou art gone
That thee I shall not celebrate
    When I remember thou wast one.

5   But yet thou canst not die, I know.
     To leave this world behind is death,
But when thou from this world wilt go,
    The whole world vapors with thy breath.

Or if, when thou, the world's soul, go'st,
10   It stay, 'tis but thy carcass then,
The fairest woman but thy ghost,
    But corrupt worms, the worthiest men.

62 **spirits** vapors emanating from the blood believed to control
the functions of the body 63 **need** are needed 72 **his** its,
i.e., love's **book** record 74 **dialogue of one** *i.e.*, the two souls
speak with one voice 8 **vapors** evaporates

O wrangling schools that search what fire
   Shall burn this world, had none the wit
Unto this knowledge to aspire,   15
   That this her fever might be it?

And yet she cannot waste by this,
   Nor long bear this torturing wrong,
For much corruption needful is
   To fuel such a fever long.   20

These burning fits but meteors be,
   Whose matter in thee is soon spent.
Thy beauty and all parts which are thee
   Are unchangeable firmament.

Yet 'twas of my mind, seising thee,   25
   Though it in thee cannot persever,
For I had rather owner be
   Of thee one hour than all else ever.

A Nocturnal upon St. Lucy's Day, Being the Shortest Day

'Tis the year's midnight, and it is the day's,
Lucy's, who scarce seven hours herself unmasks.
   The sun is spent, and now his flasks
   Send forth light squibs, no constant rays;
     The world's whole sap is sunk;   5
The general balm the hydroptic earth hath drunk,
Whither, as to the bed's feet, life is shrunk,
Dead and interred; yet all these seem to laugh
Compared with me, who am their epitaph.

13 **schools** the medieval universities and their scholars **fire the** conflagration expected to destroy the world just before the Day of Judgment   14 **wit** intelligence   21 **meteors** (temporary) appearances in the air   24 **firmament** the heavens (considered, unlike the earth, immune to change)   25 **'twas** *i.e.,* the fever was **seising** possessing **St. Lucy's Day** 13 December 3 **flasks** *i.e.,* of powder 4 **squibs** flashes 6 **balm** the moisture inherent in all living things and imparting vitality to them **hydroptic** thirsty

10   Study me then, you who shall lovers be
        At the next world (that is, at the next spring),
            For I am every dead thing,
            In whom Love wrought new alchemy;
                For his art did express
15   A quintessence even from nothingness,
        From dull privations and lean emptiness.
        He ruined me, and I am re-begot
        Of absence, darkness, death: things which are not.

        All others from all things draw all that's good:
20   Life, soul, form, spirit, whence they being have;
            I, by love's limbec, am the grave
            Of all that's nothing. Oft a flood
                Have we two wept, and so
        Drowned the whole world—us two. Oft did we grow
25   To be two chaoses when we did show
        Care to aught else; and often absences
        Withdrew our souls and made us carcasses.

        But I am by her death (which word wrongs her)
        Of the first nothing the elixir grown;
30   Were I a man, that I were one
            I needs must know; I should prefer,
                If I were any beast,
        Some ends, some means; yea plants, yea stones detest
        And love; all, all some properties invest;
35   If I an ordinary nothing were,
        As shadow, a light and body must be here.

        But I am none; nor will my sun renew.
        You lovers, for whose sake the lesser sun
            At this time to the Goat is run
40   To fetch new lust and give it you,
                Enjoy your summer all.

14 **express** press out   21 **limbec** alembic, that which distills
and refines   25 **chaoses** (antithetical to **world** = ordered mat-
ter)   25-26 **show Care** pay attention   28 **wrongs her** (be-
cause her (assumed?) death is physical only)   29 **first nothing**
the chaos out of which God made the creation   **elixir** quintes-
sence   34 **invest** endow   36 **As** such as   37 **my sun** *i.e.*, the
lady   39 **Goat** the sign of the zodiac called Capricorn (goats
are notoriously lustful)

Since she enjoys her long night's festival,
Let me prepare towards her, and let me call
This hour her vigil and her eve, since this
Both the year's and the day's deep midnight is.   **45**

A Lecture upon the Shadow

Stand still, and I will read to thee
A lecture, love, in love's philosophy.
These three hours that we have spent
Walking here, two shadows went
Along with us, which we ourselves produced;   **5**
But, now the sun is just above our head,
We do those shadows tread,
And to brave clearness all things are reduced.
So whilst our infant loves did grow,
Disguises did, and shadows, flow   **10**
From us and our cares; but now 'tis not so.

That love hath not attained the high'st degree
Which is still diligent lest others see.

Except our loves at this noon stay,
We shall new shadows make the other way.   **15**
As the first were made to blind
Others, these which come behind
Will work upon ourselves and blind our eyes.
If our loves faint and westwardly decline,
To me thou falsely thine,   **20**
And I to thee mine actions shall disguise.
The morning shadows wear away,
But these grow longer all the day.
But oh, love's day is short if love decay!

Love is a growing or full constant light,   **25**
And his first minute after noon is night.

42 **festival** *i.e.*, death   43 **towards her** *i.e.*, to join her   44
vigil watch kept on the eve of a festival   8 **brave** brilliant   10
Disguises false appearances   **shadows** delusions   19 **faint** wane
20 **thine** your actions

Love's Growth

I scarce believe my love to be so pure
    As I had thought it was,
    Because it doth endure
Vicissitude and season as the grass.
5   Methinks I lied all winter when I swore
My love was infinite, if spring make it more.

But if this medicine, love, which cures all sorrow
    With more, not only be no quintessence,
    But mixed of all stuffs paining soul or sense,
10   And of the sun his working vigor borrow,
Love's not so pure and abstract as they use
To say which have no mistress but their muse;
But as all else, being elemented too,
Love sometimes would contémplate, sometimes do.

15   And yet no greater, but more eminent,
    Love by the spring is grown,
    As in the firmament
Stars by the sun are not enlarged, but shown.
Gentle love-deeds, as blossoms on a bough,
20   From love's awakened root do bud out now.

If, as in water stirred more circles be
    Produced by one, love such additions take,
    Those like so many spheres but one heaven make,
For they are all concentric unto thee.
25   And though each spring do add to love new heat,
As princes do in times of action get
New taxes and remit them not in peace,
No winter shall abate the spring's increase.

8 quintessence sovereign remedy, highly refined essence 13
elemented composed of elements, "mixed of all stuffs" 15
eminent noteworthy 18 shown lighted up 24 concentric (as
the spheres are to the earth) 26 action *i.e.*, war

The Good-Morrow

I wonder, by my troth, what thou and I
   Did till we loved? Were we not weaned till then,
But sucked on country pleasures childishly?
   Or snorted we in the seven sleepers' den?
'Twas so; but this, all pleasures fancies be.   5
If ever any beauty I did see
Which I desired, and got, 'twas but a dream of thee.

And now good morrow to our waking souls,
   Which watch not one another out of fear;
For love all love of other sights controls,   10
   And makes one little room an everywhere.
Let sea-discoverers to new worlds have gone,
Let maps to other, worlds on worlds have shown,
Let us possess one world: each hath one, and is one.

My face in thine eye, thine in mine appears,   15
   And true plain hearts do in the faces rest.
Where can we find two better hemispheres,
   Without sharp north, without declining west?
Whatever dies was not mixed equally;
If our two loves be one, or thou and I   20
Love so alike that none do slacken, none can die.

The Sun Rising

   Busy old fool, unruly sun,
     Why dost thou thus
Through windows and through curtains call on us?
Must to thy motions lovers' seasons run?

3 **sucked** suckled   4 **seven sleepers** noble youths of Ephesus who, taking refuge from persecution in a cave, slept for 230 years   5 **but** except   10 **controls** overmasters   13 **other** others 14 **is one** *i.e.*, man is the microcosm, a little world   16 **rest** *i.e.*, show themselves   18 **sharp north** *i.e.*, cold **declining west** *i.e.*, change   19 **Whatever . . . equally** a "law" of Renaissance physics (**dies** = decays)

5   Saucy, pedantic wretch, go chide
             Late schoolboys and sour prentices,
          Go tell court huntsmen that the king will ride,
          Call country ants to harvest offices.
        Love, all alike, no season knows nor clime,
10   Nor hours, days, months, which are the rags of time.

             Thy beams, so reverend and strong
               Why shouldst thou think?
          I could eclipse and cloud them with a wink,
          But that I would not lose her sight so long.
15   If her eyes have not blinded thine,
             Look, and tomorrow late tell me
          Whether both the Indias of spice and mine
          Be where thou left'st them, or lie here with me;
        Ask for those kings whom thou saw'st yesterday,
20   And thou shalt hear: all here in one bed lay.

             She is all states, and all princes I;
               Nothing else is.
          Princes do but play us; compared to this,
          All honor's mimic, all wealth alchemy.
25   Thou, sun, art half as happy as we
             In that the world's contracted thus;
          Thine age asks ease, and since thy duties be
          To warm the world, that's done in warming us.
        Shine here to us, and thou art everywhere;
30   This bed thy center is, these walls thy sphere.

The Dream

Dear love, for nothing less than thee
Would I have broke this happy dream
         It was a theme

---

9 **all alike** unchanging   13 **wink** closing of the eye   17 **both the Indias** the East Indies, which exported spices, and the West Indies, which exported precious metals   23 **play** impersonate   24 **alchemy** *i.e.,* imposture   27 **asks** requires   30 **sphere** (the sun, like other planets, was thought of as part of a hollow globe revolving round the earth)

For reason, much too strong for fantasy;
    Therefore thou wakedst me wisely. Yet   5
My dream thou brok'st not, but continuedst it;
Thou art so truth that thoughts of thee suffice
To make dreams truths, and fables histories.
Enter these arms, for since thou thought'st it best
Not to dream all my dream, let's act the rest.   10

    As lightning or a taper's light,
    Thine eyes and not thy noise waked me.
          Yet I thought thee
(For thou lov'st truth) an angel at first sight;
    But when I saw thou saw'st my heart,   15
And knew'st my thoughts (beyond an angel's art),
When thou knew'st what I dreamt, when thou knew'st
    when
Excess of joy would wake me, and cam'st then,
I must confess it could not choose but be
Profane to think thee anything but thee.   20

    Coming and staying showed thee, thee,
    But rising makes me doubt that now
          Thou art not thou.
That love is weak where fear's as strong as he.
    'Tis not all spirit, pure and brave,   25
If mixture it of fear, shame, honor have.
Perchance as torches which must ready be,
Men light and put out, so thou deal'st with me:
Thou cam'st to kindle, go'st to come; then I
Will dream that hope again, but else would die.   30

The Anniversary

    All kings and all their favorites,
    All glory of honors, beauties, wits,
    The sun itself, which makes times as they pass,

4 reason (which does not work during sleep) **fantasy im-
agination**   **8 histories** *i.e.,* true stories   **9 best** *i.e.,* best for me
11 as lightning or light sometimes wakes a sleeper   **16 beyond
. . . art** *i.e.,* to read someone's thoughts is more than an angel
can do   **22 doubt** fear   **25 all spirit** purely spiritual   **3 makes
times** *i.e.,* measures time

Is elder by a year now than it was
5   When thou and I first one another saw.
All other things to their destruction draw;
    Only our love hath no decay;
This, no tomorrow hath nor yesterday;
Running, it never runs from us away,
10 But truly keeps his first, last, everlasting day.

Two graves must hide thine and my corse.
If one might, death were no divorce.
Alas, as well as other princes, we
(Who prince enough in one another be)
15   Must leave at last in death these eyes and ears,
Oft fed with true oaths and with sweet salt tears;
    But souls where nothing dwells but love
(All other thoughts being inmates) then shall prove
This, or a love increasèd there above,
When bodies to their graves, souls from their graves, re-
20   move.

And then we shall be throughly blest,
But we no more than all the rest.
Here upon earth we are kings, and none but we
Can be such kings, nor of such, subjects be.
25   Who is so safe as we, where none can do
Treason to us, except one of us two?
    True and false fears let us refrain,
Let us love nobly, and live, and add again
Years and years unto years till we attain
30 To write threescore.—This is the second of our reign.

The Canonization

For God's sake hold your tongue and let me love!
    Or chide my palsy or my gout,
My five grey hairs or ruined fortune flout;
With wealth your state, your mind with arts improve,
5   Take you a course, get you a place,
        Observe his honor or his grace,
    Or the king's real or his stampèd face

18 **inmates** lodgers, strangers   **prove** learn by experience, find
21 **then** *i.e.,* in heaven, where the blessed are all equally happy
throughly thoroughly   24 **of such** *i.e.,* of such kings   27 **re-
frain** repress, shun   2 **Or** either   4 **arts** studies   5 **Take . . .
course** take steps   7 **stampèd** face (on coins)

Contemplate, what you will approve,
    So you will let me love.

Alas, alas, who's injured by my love?   10
    What merchant ships have my sighs drowned?
Who says my tears have overflowed his ground?
When did my colds a forward spring remove?
    When did the heats which my veins fill
    Add one more to the plaguy bill?   15
Soldiers find wars, and lawyers find out still
    Litigious men which quarrels move,
      Though she and I do love.

Call us what you will, we are made such by love.
    Call her one, me another fly,   20
We are tapers too, and at our own cost die;
And we in us find the eagle and the dove.
    The phoenix riddle hath more wit
    By us; we two being one, are it.
So to one neutral thing both sexes fit,   25
    We die and rise the same, and prove
      Mysterious by this love.

We can die by it, if not live by love,
    And if unfit for tombs and hearse
Our legend be, it will be fit for verse;   30
And if no piece of chronicle we prove,
    We'll build in sonnets pretty rooms:
    As well a well-wrought urn becomes
The greatest ashes as half-acre tombs,
    And by these hymns all shall approve   35
      Us canonized for love,

8 **approve** try out, take your pick of   9 **So** if only   13 **forward** early   15 **plaguy bill** weekly summary of deaths especially those from the plague   17 **quarrels** law-suits   20 **fly** *i.e.*, moth, which is attracted to flame and burns in it   22 **eagle** *i.e.*, strength, rapacity   **dove** *i.e.*, mildness   24 **phoenix riddle** the anomaly of the life-history of the phoenix, only one specimen living at any time   **wit** meaning   31 **chronicle** history   32 **sonnets** poems of love   **rooms** (Italian *stanza* = room)   33 **becomes** befits   35 **approve** affirm

And thus invoke us: "You whom reverend love
   Made one another's hermitage,
You to whom love was peace, that now is rage,
40 Who did the whole world's soul contract, and drove
   Into the glasses of your eyes
   (So made such mirrors and such spies
That they did all to you epitomize)
   Countries, towns, courts: beg from above
45   A pattern of your love!"

The Computation

For the first twenty years since yesterday
I scarce believed thou couldst be gone away;
For forty more I fed on favors past,
And forty on hopes that thou wouldst they might last.
5 Tears drowned one hundred, and sighs blew out two,
A thousand, I did neither think nor do,
Or not divide, all being one thought of you,
Or in a thousand more forgot that too.
Yet call not this long life, but think that I
10 Am, by being dead, immortal. Can ghosts die?

The Undertaking

I have done one braver thing
   Than all the worthies did,
And yet a braver thence doth spring,
   Which is, to keep that hid.

5   It were but madness now to impart
   The skill of specular stone,

37 **invoke** pray to as saints   40 **contract** epitomize **drove**
crammed   41 **glasses** eyeballs   45 **pattern** model from which
copies can be made   **The Undertaking** entitled *Platonic Love*
in some manuscripts   1 **braver** more wonderful   2 **worthies**
(nine) great men of ancient history and legend   5 **impart**
make known   6 **skill of specular stone** the art of cutting trans-
parent gypsum into thin sheets; the stone was unknown in
Europe and believed no longer to exist

When he which can have learned the art
  To cut it can find none.

So, if I now should utter this,
  Others (because no more   10
Such stuff to work upon there is)
  Would love but as before.

But he who loveliness within
  Hath found, all outward loathes,
For he who color loves, and skin,   15
  Loves but their oldest clothes.

If as I have, you also do
  Virtue attired in woman see,
And dare love that, and say so too,
  And forget the he and she,   20

And if this love, though placèd so,
  From profane men you hide,
Which will no faith on this bestow,
  Or if they do, deride,

Then you have done a braver thing   25
  Than all the worthies did;
And a braver thence will spring,
  Which is, to keep that hid.

The Funeral

Whoever comes to shroud me, do not harm
        Nor question much
That subtle wreath of hair which crowns my arm;
The mystery, the sign, you must not touch,
        For 'tis my outward soul,   5
Viceroy to that, which then to heaven being gone,
        Will leave this to control
And keep these limbs, her provinces, from dissolutión.

9 **utter** disclose **this** "one braver thing"   18 **attired** incorpo-
rated   21 **placed so** fixed in such a manner   1 **shroud** lay out
for burial   3 **subtle** thin, fine   8 **her** *i.e.*, the soul's

For if the sinewy thread my brain lets fall
10   Through every part
Can tie those parts and make me one of all,
These hairs, which upward grew, and strength and art
          Have, from a better brain,
Can better do it; except she meant that I
15   By this should know my pain,
As prisoners then are manacled, when they are con-
          demned to die.

Whate'er she meant by it, bury it with me,
          For since I am
Love's martyr, it might breed idolatry
20 If into others' hands these relics came.
          As 'twas humility
To afford to it all that a soul can do,
          So 'tis some bravery
That since you would save none of me, I bury some of
          you.

The Relic

When my grave is broke up again
Some second guest to entertain
(For graves have learned that womanhead
To be to more than one a bed)
5   And he that digs it spies
A bracelet of bright hair about the bone,
          Will he not let us alone,
And think that there a loving couple lies,
Who thought that this device might be some way
10 To make their souls at the last busy day
Meet at this grave, and make a little stay?

          If this fall in a time or land
          Where mis-devotion doth command,
          Then he that digs us up will bring

9 **sinewy thread** the nervous system   14 **she** *i.e.*, the lady who
gave him the bracelet of hair   22 **afford** attribute   23 **some
bravery** a kind of defiance   3 **womanhead** womanhood, habit
of women   10 **last busy day** day of resurrection   12 **fall** hap-
pens

Us to the bishop and the king   15
   To make us relics; then
Thou shalt be a Mary Magdalen, and I
   A something else thereby.
All women shall adore us, and some men;
And since at such time miracles are sought,   20
I would have that age by this paper taught
What miracles we harmless lovers wrought:

   First, we loved well and faithfully,
   Yet knew not what we loved, nor why;
   Difference of sex no more we knew   25
   Than our guardian angels do;
      Coming and going, we
Perchance might kiss, but not between those meals;
   Our hands ne'er touched the seals
Which nature, injured by late law, sets free.   30
These miracles we did; but now, alas,
All measure and all language I should pass,
Should I tell what a miracle she was.

Twickenham Garden

Blasted with sighs and surrounded with tears,
   Hither I come to seek the spring,
   And at mine eyes, and at mine ears,
Receive such balms as else cure everything;
   But oh, self-traitor, I do bring   5
The spider love, which transubstantiates all,
   And can convert manna to gall;
And that this place may thoroughly be thought
True Paradise, I have the serpent brought.

'Twere wholesomer for me that winter did   10
   Benight the glory of this place,
   And that a grave frost did forbid
These trees to laugh and mock me to my face;

29-30 seals Which nature . . . sets free prohibitions unknown
to nature   30 late law man-made law (and therefore not as
old as the law of nature)   32 pass exceed   1 surrounded
overflown   6 transubstantiates changes the substance of

But that I may not this disgrace
15   Endure, nor leave this garden, Love, let me
      Some senseless piece of this place be:
Make me a mandrake so I may groan here,
Or a stone fountain weeping out my year.

Hither with crystal vials, lovers, come,
20   And take my tears, which are love's wine,
       And try your mistress' tears at home,
For all are false that taste not just like mine.
      Alas! hearts do not in eyes shine,
Nor can you more judge woman's thoughts by tears,
25   Than by her shadow what she wears.
O perverse sex, where none is true but she
Who's therefore true because her truth kills me.

17 **mandrake** a plant whose root was thought to resemble the
human body and to shriek or groan when pulled up   21 **try**
test

ELEGIES

※

Elegy III

Change

Although thy hand and faith, and good works too,
Have sealed thy love, which nothing should undo,
Yea though thou fall back, that apostasy
Confirm thy love, yet much, much I fear thee.
Women are like the arts, forced unto none,   5
Open to all searchers, unprized if unknown.
If I have caught a bird and let him fly,
Another fowler, using these means as I,
May catch the same bird; and as these things be,
Women are made for men, not him, nor me.   10
Foxes and goats, all beasts, change when they please.
Shall women, more hot, wily, wild than these,
Be bound to one man, and did nature then
Idly make them apter to endure than men?
They're our clogs, not their own; if a man be   15
Chained to a galley, yet the galley's free.
Who hath a plowland casts all his seed corn there,
And yet allows his ground more corn should bear;
Though Danuby into the sea must flow,
The sea receives the Rhine, Volga, and Po.   20
By nature, which gave it, this liberty
Thou lov'st, but oh! canst thou love it and me?
Likeness glues love; and if that so thou do,
To make us 'like, and love, must I change too?
More than thy hate, I hate it. Rather let me   25
Allow her change than change as oft as she,
And so not teach, but force my opinión

2 **sealed** ratified, attested   5 **forced unto none** compulsory for
none 6 **unprized** unvalued 8 **these** the same 14 **Idly** point-
lessly 18 **more corn** *i.e.*, that which grows from any seed
falling on his land by chance

To love not any one, nor every one.
To live in one land is captivity,
30   To run all countries a wild roguery;
Waters stink soon if in one place they bide,
And in the vast sea are more putrefied;
But when they kiss one bank, and leaving this,
Never look back, but the next bank do kiss,
35   Then are they purest. Change is the nursery
Of music, joy, life, and eternity.

ELEGY IV

The Perfume

Once, and but once, found in thy company,
All thy supposed escapes are laid on me,
And as a thief at bar is questioned there
By all the men that have been robbed that year,
5   So am I (by this traitorous means surprised)
By thy hydroptic father catechized.
Though he had wont to search with glazèd eyes
As though he came to kill a cockatrice,
Though he have oft sworn that he would remove
10   Thy beauty's beauty and food of our love,
Hope of his goods, if I with thee were seen,
Yet close and secret as our souls we've been.
Though thy immortal mother, which doth lie
Still buried in her bed, yet will not die,
15   Take this advantage to sleep out daylight
And watch thy entries and returns all night,
And when she takes thy hand and would seem kind,
Doth search what rings and armlets she can find,
And kissing, notes the color of thy face,
20   And fearing lest thou art swol'n doth thee embrace,
And to try if thou long, doth name strange meats,
And notes thy paleness, blushings, sighs, and sweats,

30 **roguery** vagrancy   32 **putrefied** made salty   2 **escapes** es-
capades   6 **hydroptic** dropsical   7 **glazèd** closed   8 **cockatrice**
a serpent whose look was supposed to kill (it would therefore
be fatal to look it in the eye)   14 **still** always

And politicly will to thee confess
The sins of her own youth's rank lustiness,
Yet love these sorceries did remove, and move   25
Thee to gull thine own mother for my love.
Thy little brethren, which like fairy sprites
Oft skipped into our chamber those sweet nights;
And, kissed and ingled on thy father's knee,
Were bribed next day to tell what they did see;   30
The grim eight-foot-high iron-bound servingman,
That oft names God in oaths, and only than,
He that to bar the first gate doth as wide
As the great Rhodián Colossus stride,
Which, if in hell no other pains there were,   35
Makes me fear hell because he must be there,
Though by thy father he were hired to this,
Could never witness any touch or kiss.
But oh, too common ill, I brought with me
That which betrayed me to mine enemy: 40
A loud perfume, which at mine entrance cried
Even at thy father's nose. So were we spied;
When, like a tyrant king that in his bed
Smelt gunpowder, the pale wretch shiverèd.
Had it been some bad smell, he would have thought   45
That his own feet or breath that smell had wrought,
But as we, in our isle imprisonèd,
Where cattle only and divers dogs are bred,
The precious unicorns strange monsters call,
So thought he good strange—that had none at all.   50
I taught my silks their whistling to forbear;
Even my oppressed shoes dumb and speechless were;
Only thou, bitter-sweet, whom I had laid
Next me, me traitorously hast betrayed,
And unsuspected hast invisibly   55
At once fled unto him and stayed with me.
Base excrement of earth, which dost confound

---

23 **politicly** craftily, as a stratagem   26 **gull** deceive   29 **ingled**
fondled   31 **iron-bound** armed   32 **than** then   47 **isle** *i.e.,*
Britain   49 **precious** (because their horns were used medicin-
ally)   50 **good** *i.e.,* a good odor   52 **oppressed** (by the feet)
57 **excrement** outgrowth   **confound** confuse and prevent (sick-
rooms were fumigated with perfume)

Sense from distinguishing the sick from sound,
By thee the silly amorous sucks his death,
60   By drawing in a leprous harlot's breath;
By thee the greatest stain to man's estate
Falls on us, to be called effeminate.
Though you be much loved in the prince's hall,
There, things that seem exceed substantial.
65   Gods, when ye fumed on altars, were pleased well
Because you were burnt, not that they liked your smell;
You're loathsome all, being taken simply alone.
Shall we love ill things joined, and hate each one?
If you were good, your good doth soon decay;
'0   And you are rare, that takes the good away.
All my perfumes I give most willingly
To embalm thy father's corse. What? will he die?

Elegy V

His Picture

Here take my picture. Though I bid farewell,
Thine in my heart, where my soul dwells, shall dwell.
'Tis like me now, but I dead, 'twill be more,
When we are shadows both, than 'twas before.
5   When weather-beaten I come back, my hand
Perhaps with rude oars torn, or sunbeams tanned,
My face and breast of haircloth, and my head
With care's rash, sudden hoariness o'erspread,
My body a sack of bones, broken within,
10   And powder's blue stains scattered on my skin,
If rival fools tax thee to have loved a man
So foul and coarse as, oh, I may seem than,
This shall say what I was, and thou shalt say,

---

64 **substantial** *i.e.*, substantial things, things that have sub-
stance   65 **ye** *i.e.*, perfume   **fumed** smoked   67 **simply** indi-
vidually (a perfume is a compound of loathsome elements)   69
decay waste away, *i.e.*, evaporate   70 **And if**   6 **Perhaps . . .
torn** (if he should be captured and condemned to the galleys)
7 **of haircloth** *i.e.*, hairy   8 **rash** quickly effected   11 **tax** blame
12 **foul** ugly   **than** then

"Do his hurts reach me? doth my worth decay?
Or do they reach his judging mind that he   15
Should now love less what he did love to see?
That which in him was fair and delicate
Was but the milk which in love's childish state
Did nurse it, who now is grown strong enough
To feed on that which to disusèd tastes seems tough."   20

ELEGY IX

The Autumal

No spring nor summer beauty hath such grace
As I have seen in one autumnal face.
Young beauties force our love, and that's a rape;
This doth but counsel, yet you cannot 'scape.
If 'twere a shame to love, here 'twere no shame;   5
Affection here takes reverence's name.
Were her first years the golden age? That's true,
But now she's gold oft tried and ever new.
That was her torrid and inflaming time;
This is her tolerable tropic clime.   10
Fair eyes! Who asks more heat than comes from hence,
He in a fever wishes pestilence.
Call not these wrinkles graves; if graves they were,
They were Love's graves, for else he is nowhere.
Yet lies not Love dead here, but here doth sit   15
Vowed to this trench like an anchorite;
And here, till hers, which must be his death, come,
He doth not dig a grave, but build a tomb.
Here dwells he; though he sojourn ev'rywhere
In progress, yet his standing-house is here,   20
Here, where still evening is, not noon nor night,
Where no voluptuousness, yet all delight.
In all her words, unto all hearers fit,

18 **milk** (cf. Hebrews v. 13: "every one that useth milk . . .
is a babe")   20 **disused** unaccustomed   7 **golden age** the first
age of the world, when mankind was untroubled by want or
crime   8 **tried** purified   10 **tropic** *i.e.*, temperate   16 **anchorite**
hermit   20 **progress** round of visits (by royalty)   **standing-
house** permanent residence   21 **still** always

You may at revels, you at council, sit.
25 This is Love's timber, youth his underwood;
There he, as wine in June, enrages blood,
Which then comes seasonabliest when our taste
And appetite to other things is past.
Xerxes' strange Lydian love, the platan tree,
30 Was loved for age, none being so large as she,
Or else because, being young, nature did bless
Her youth with age's glory, barrenness.
If we love things long sought, age is a thing
Which we are fifty years in compassing;
35 If transitory things which soon decay,
Age must be loveliest at the latest day.
    But name not winter faces, whose skin's slack,
Lank as an unthrift's purse, but a soul's sack,
Whose eyes seek light within, for all here's shade,
40 Whose mouths are holes, rather worn out than made,
Whose every tooth to a several place is gone
To vex their souls at resurrectión;
Name not these living death's-heads unto me,
For these not anciént, but ántique be.
45 I hate extremes; yet I had rather stay
With tombs that cradles, to wear out a day.
Since such love's natural lation is, may still
My love descend and journey down the hill,
Not panting after growing beauties. So
50 I shall ebb on with them who homeward go.

Elegy X

The Dream

Image of her (whom I love more than she
    Whose fair impression in my faithful heart

24 revels gay parties   25 underwood undergrowth   28 to for
29 platan plane (Xerxes, finding a magnificent plane tree in
Lydia, set a guard over it)   35 If i.e., if we love   38 Lank
hollow   41 several different   42 resurrection (when the body
rejoins the soul and its parts must be collected)   47 lation
motion   1 Image (presumably a picture)

Makes me her medal, and makes her love me
    As kings do coins to which their stamps impart
The value), go, and take my heart from hence,   5
    Which now is grown too great and good for me.
Honors oppress weak spirits, and our sense
    Strong objects dull; the more, the less we see.

When you are gone, and reason gone with you,
    Then fantasy is queen, and soul, and all;   10
She can present joys meaner than you do,
    Convenient and more proportional.
So if I dream I have you, I have you,
    For all our joys are but fantastical.
And so I 'scape the pain, for pain is true;   15
    And sleep, which locks up sense, doth lock out all.

After a such fruition I shall wake,
    And, but the waking, nothing shall repent,
And shall to Love more thankful sonnets make
    Than if more honor, tears, and pains were spent.   20
But, dearest heart, and dearer image, stay;
    Alas, true joys at best are dream enough;
Though you stay here, you pass too fast away,
    For even at first life's taper is a snuff.

Filled with her love, may I be rather grown   25
Mad with much heart than idiot with none.

ELEGY XII

At his Mistress's Departure

Since she must go and I must mourn, come night!
Environ me with darkness whilst I write;
Shadow that hell unto me which alone
I am to suffer when my love is gone.

7 **sense** senses   10 **fantasy** imagination   11 **She** *i.e.*, fantasy
meaner more moderate   12 **proportional** appropriate (to his
weakness)   14 **fantastical** products of imagination   15 **true**
real   24 **snuff** candle-end   3 **Shadow** represent, symbolize

5   Alas! the darkest magic cannot do it;
    Thou and great hell to boot are shadows to it.
    Should Cynthia quit thee, Venus, and each star,
    It would not form one thought dark as mine are.
    I could lend thee obscureness now, and say
10 Out of my self, there should be no more day;
    Such is already my felt want of sight,
    Did not the fires within me force a light.
       O Love, that fire and darkness should be mixed,
    Or to thy triumphs so strange torments fixed!
15 Is't because thou thyself art blind that we,
    Thy martyrs, must no more each other see?
    Or tak'st thou pride to break us on the wheel,
    And view old chaos in the pains we feel?
    Or have we left undone some mutual rite
20 Through holy fear, that merits thy despite?
    No, no. The fault was mine; impute it to me,
    Or rather to conspiring destiny,
    Which, since I loved for form before, decreed
    That I should suffer when I loved indeed.
25 And therefore now, sooner than I can say
    I saw the golden fruit, 'tis rapt away,
    Or as I had watched one drop in a vast stream,
    And I left wealthy only in a dream.
    Yet, Love, thou'rt blinder than thyself in this,
30 To vex my dove-like friend for my amiss,
    And where my own sad truth may expiate
    Thy wrath, to make her fortune run my fate.
    So blinded justice doth, when favorites fall,
    Strike them, their house, their friends, their followers all.
35 Was't not enough that thou didst dart thy fires
    Into our bloods, inflaming our desires,
    And mad'st us sigh and glow and pant and burn,
    And then thyself into our flame didst turn?
    Was't not enough that thou didst hazard us
40 To paths in love so dark, so dangerous,
    And those so ambushed round with household spies,
    And over all thy husband's towering eyes,

6 **to** compared to   7 **Cynthia** the moon   10 **Out of my self** *i.e.*,
my darkness is sufficient (to obscure day)   23 **form** fashion
26 **rapt** snatched, stolen   30 **amiss** error   32 **run** share   42
towering soaring aloft ready to strike (like a hawk)

That flamed with oily sweat of jealousy?
Yet went we not still on with constancy?
Have we not kept our guards like spy on spy?   45
Had correspondence whilst the foe stood by?
Stol'n (more to sweeten them) our many blisses
Of meetings, conference, embracements, kisses?
Shadowed with negligence our most respects?
Varied our language through all dialects   50
Of becks, winks, looks, and often under boards
Spoke dialogues with our feet, far from our words?
Have we proved all these secrets of our art,
Yea, thy pale inwards and thy panting heart?
And after all this passèd purgatory   55
Must sad divorce make us the vulgar story?
First let our eyes be riveted quite through
Our turning brains, and both our lips grow to;
Let our arms clasp like ivy, and our fear
Freeze us together that we may stick here   60
Till fortune, that would rive us, with the deed
Strain her eyes open, and it make them bleed.
For Love it cannot be (whom hitherto
I have accused) should such a mischief do.
  O fortune, thou'rt not worth my least exclaim,   65
And plague enough thou hast in thine own shame.
Do thy great worst; my friend and I have arms,
Though not against thy strokes, against thy harms.
Rend us in sunder; thou canst not divide
Our bodies so but that our souls are tied,   70
And we can love by letters still, and gifts
And thoughts and dreams; love never wanteth shifts.
I will not look upon the quick'ning sun
But straight her beauty to my sense shall run;
The air shall note her soft, the fire most pure,   75
Water suggest her clear, and the earth sure.
Time shall not lose our passages: the spring

49 **Shadowed** screened **our most respects** what mattered most
to us 51 **becks** nods 52 **far** far different 53 **proved** found
out 54 **pale inwards** pallor of mind or soul 58 **grow to** cling
together 62 **Strain her eyes open** (fortune is blind) 72
wanteth shifts is at a loss for expedients 75 **note her** indicate
that she is 76 **clear** beautiful 77 **lose our passages** forget
what we have done

How fresh our love was in the beginning,
The summer how it ripened in the ear,
80 And autumn what our golden harvests were.
The winter I'll not think on, to spite thee,
But count it a lost season—so shall she.
    And dearest friend, since we must part, drown night
With hope of day. Burthens well borne are light.
85 Though cold and darkness longer hang somewhere,
Yet Phoebus equally lights all the sphere.
And what he cannot in like portions pay
The world enjoys in mass, and so we may.
Be then ever yourself, and let no woe
90 Win on your health, your youth, your beauty; so
Declare yourself base fortune's enemy,
No less by your contempt than constancy,
That I may grow enamored on your mind
When my own thoughts I there reflected find.
95 For this to the comfort of my dear I vow:
My deeds shall still be what my words are now,
The pole shall move to teach me ere I start,
And when I change my love, I'll change my heart;
Nay, if I wax but cold in my desire,
00 Think heaven hath motion lost, and the world fire.
Much more I could, but many words have made
That oft suspected which men would persuade;
Take therefore all in this: I love so true
As I will never look for less in you.

ELEGY XVI

On his Mistress

By our first strange and fatal interview,
By all desires which thereof did ensue,
By our long starving hopes, by that remorse
Which my words' masculine, persuasive force
5   Begot in thee, and by the memory

85 somewhere in certain places 87 in like portions pay appor-
tion 90 Win on encroach upon, impair 97 start swerve,
withdraw 99 wax grow 1 interview view of each other 3
remorse pity

Of hurts which spies and rivals threatened me,
I calmly beg; but by thy parents' wrath,
By all pains which want and divorcement hath,
I conjure thee; and all the oaths which I
And thou have sworn to seal joint constancy,   10
Here I unswear, and overswear them thus:
Thou shalt not love by ways so dangerous.
Temper, O fair love, love's impetuous rage;
Be my true mistress still, not my feigned page.
I'll go, and by thy kind leave, leave behind   15
Thee, only worthy to nurse in my mind
Thirst to come back. Oh, if thou die before,
My soul from other lands to thee shall soar.
Thy (else almighty) beauty cannot move
Rage from the seas, nor thy love teach them love,   20
Nor tame wild Boreas' harshness. Thou hast read
How roughly he in pieces shiverèd
Fair Orithyia, whom he swore he loved.
Fall ill or good, 'tis madness to have proved
Dangers unurged. Feed on this flattery: 25
That absent lovers one in the other be.
Dissemble nothing, not a boy, nor change
Thy body's habit, nor mind's; be not strange
To thyself only; all will spy in thy face
A blushing, womanly, discovering grace.   30
Richly clothed apes are called apes, and as soon
Eclipsed as bright, we call the moon the moon.
Men of France, changeable chameleons,
Spitals of diseases, shops of fashions,
Love's fuelers, and the rightest company   35
Of players which upon the world's stage be,
Will quickly know thee, and no less, alas!
The indifferent Italian, as we pass
His warm land, well content to think thee page,

8 **divorcement** separation   11 **overswear** outswear   19 **move** remove   21 **Boreas** the north wind   23 **Orithyia** a Thracian maiden abducted by Boreas and destroyed by his violent love-making   24 **Fall ill or good** whether ill or good befalls   **proved** experienced, undergone   27 **dissemble** pretend to be   30 **discovering** revealing   34 **Spitals** hospitals *i.e.*, masses   35 **rightest** truest, most genuine   37 **know** (1) recognize, (2) have carnal knowledge of   38 **indifferent** not particular, apt for all vices

40   Will hunt thee with such lust and hideous rage
        As Lot's fair guests were vexed. But none of these,
        Nor spongy, hydroptic Dutch shall thee displease
        If thou stay here. Oh stay here; for, for thee,
        England is only a worthy gallery
45   To walk in expectation, till from thence
        Our greatest king call thee to his presence.
        When I am gone, dream me some happiness,
        Nor let thy looks our long-hid love confess,
        Nor praise nor dispraise me, nor bless nor curse
50   Openly love's force, nor in bed fright thy nurse
        With midnight's startings, crying out, "O! O
        Nurse! Oh! my love is slain! I saw him go
        O'er the white Alps alone; I saw him, I,
        Assailed, fight, taken, stabbed, bleed, fall, and die."
55   Augur me better chance, except dread Jove
        Think it enough for me to have had thy love.

Elegy XIX

To his Mistress Going to Bed

        Come, madam, come! All rest my powers defy;
        Until I labor, I in labor lie.
        The foe ofttimes, having the foe in sight,
        Is tired with standing though he never fight.
5   Off with that girdle, like heaven's zone glittering,
        But a far fairer world encompassing.
        Unpin that spangled breastplate, which you wear
        That the eyes of busy fools may be stopped there.
        Unlace yourself, for that harmonious chime
10   Tells me from you that now it is bedtime.
        Off with that happy busk, which I envý,
        That still can be, and still can stand so nigh.
        Your gown, going off, such beauteous state reveals
        As when from flow'ry meads the hill's shadow steals.

41 **guests** the angel visitors whom the Sodomites solicited
(Genesis xix)   42 **hydroptic** insatiably thirsty (for beer)   44
England is only only England is   **gallery** promenade   5 **zone**
(Latin *zona* = girdle)   9 **chime** the noise made by the laces
passing through the eyelets   11 **busk** corset

Off with that wiry coronet, and show 15
The hairy diadem which on you doth grow.
Off with those shoes you wear, and safely tread
In this, Love's hallowed temple, this soft bed.
In such white robes heaven's angels used to be
Received by men; thou, angel, bring'st with thee 20
A heaven like Mahomet's paradise. And though
Ill spirits walk in white, we eas'ly know
By this these angels from an evil sprite:
Those set our hairs, but these our flesh upright.

License my roving hands and let them go 25
Before, behind, between, above, below.
O my America, my new-found land!
My kingdom, safeliest when with one man manned,
My mine of precious stones, my empery,
How blest am I in this discovering thee! 30
To enter in these bonds is to be free;
Then where my hand is set, my seal shall be.

Full nakedness, all joys are due to thee!
As souls unbodied, bodies unclothed must be
To taste whole joys. Gems which you women use 35
Are like Atlanta's balls, cast in men's views
That when a fool's eye lighteth on a gem,
His earthly soul may covet theirs, not them.
Like pictures, or like books' gay coverings made
For laymen, are all women thus arrayed; 40
Themselves are mystic books, which only we
Whom their imputed grace will dignify
Must see revealed. Then, since that I may know,
As liberally as to a midwife show
Thyself. Cast all, yea, this white linen hence; 45
Here is no penance, much less innocence.

To teach thee, I am naked first. Why than,
What need'st thou have more covering than a man?

15 **coronet** headdress   29 **empery** empire   34 **unbodied** re-
leased from the body   36 **Atlanta's balls** (which Atalanta threw
behind her to detain competitors in foot-races)   38 **earthly**
earth-bound   **theirs** *i.e.,* their gems   42 **imputed** (theologi-
cally, all grace is imputed)   46 **penance** (sometimes performed
in a white gown)   47 **than** then

SATIRES

Satire III

Kind pity chokes my spleen; brave scorn forbids
Those tears to issue which swell my eyelids;
I must not laugh, nor weep sins and be wise.
May railing, then, cure these worn maladies?
5 Is not our mistress, fair Religión,
As worthy of all our soul's devotión
As virtue was to the first, blinded age?
Are not heaven's joys as valiant to assuage
Lusts as earth's honor was to them? Alas,
10 As we do them in means, shall they surpass
Us in the end? And shall thy father's spirit
Meet blind philosophers in heaven, whose merit
Of strict life may be imputed faith, and hear
Thee, whom he taught so easy ways and near
15 To follow, damned? Oh, if thou dar'st, fear this.
This fear great courage and high valor is.
Dar'st thou aid mutinous Dutch, and dar'st thou lay
Thee in ships, wooden sepulchers, a prey
To leaders' rage, to storms, to shot, to dearth?
20 Dar'st thou dive seas and dungeons of the earth?
Hast thou courageous fire to thaw the ice
Of frozen north discoveries? And thrice
Colder than salamanders, like divine
Children in the oven, fires of Spain and the line,
25 Whose countries limbecs to our bodies be,

1 **spleen** the seat of morose feelings 3 **weep** shed tears over
4 **worn** worn-out, venerable 7 **the first, blinded** age the pre-
Christian era 10 **means** (by virtue of the Christian revelation)
13 **imputed** accredited as 15 **this** *i.e.*, damnation 17 **mu-
tinous Dutch** (in revolt against their Spanish overlords) 20
dive plow through 24 **children** the three Jews cast into a
fiery furnace by Nebuchadnezzar (Daniel iii) **fires of Spain**
i.e., of the Inquisition **line** equator 25 **limbecs** vessels used
in distillation, retorts

Canst thou for gain bear? and must every he
Which cries not "goddess!" to thy mistress, draw,
Or eat thy poisonous words? Courage of straw!
O desperate coward, wilt thou seem bold, and
To thy foes and His who made thee, to stand   30
Sentinel in His world's garrison, thus yield
And for forbidden wars leave th' appointed field?
Know thy foes: the foul devil, whom thou
Striv'st to please, for hate, not love, would allow
Thee fain his whole realm, to be quit; and as   35
The world's all parts wither away and pass,
So the world's self, thy other loved foe, is
In her decrepit wane, and thou, loving this,
Dost love a withered and worn strumpet; last,
Flesh (itself's death) and joys which flesh can taste   40
Thou lov'st, and thy fair, goodly soul, which doth
Give this flesh power to taste joy, thou dost loathe.
    Seek true religion. O where? Mirreus,
Thinking her unhoused here and fled from us,
Seeks her at Rome, there, because he doth know   45
That she was there a thousand years ago;
He loves her rags so, as we here obey
The state-cloth where the prince sat yesterday.
Crantz to such brave loves will not be enthralled,
But loves her only who at Geneva is called   50
Religion, plain, simple, sullen, young,
Contemptuous, yet unhandsome; as among
Lecherous humors there is one that judges
No wenches wholesome but coarse country drudges.
Graius stays still at home here, and because   55
Some preachers (vile ambitious bawds) and laws,
Still new like fashions, bid him think that she
Which dwells with us is only perfect, he
Embraceth her whom his godfathers will
Tender to him, being tender, as wards still   60
Take such wives as their guardians offer, or
Pay values. Careless Phrygius doth abhor
All, because all cannot be good, as one,

27 draw *i.e.,* your sword 35 fain gladly be quit do away
with, destroy (you) 38 wane decline 47 obey bow to 48
state-cloth cloth covering the throne 49 brave magnificent 55
still ever 57 Still always 62 values compensation

Knowing some women whores, dares marry none.
65 Graccus loves all as one, and thinks that so
As women do in divers countries go
In divers habits, yet are still one kind,
So doth, so is Religion; and this blind-
ness too much light breeds. But unmoved thou
70 Of force must one, and forced, but one allow,
And the right—ask thy father which is she.
Let him ask his. Though truth and falsehood be
Near twins, yet truth a little elder is.
Be busy to seek her; believe me this:
75 He's not of none, nor worst, that seeks the best.
To adore or scorn an image, or protest,
May all be bad. Doubt wisely; in strange way
To stand inquiring right is not to stray;
To sleep or run wrong is. On a huge hill,
80 Cragged and steep, truth stands, and he that will
Reach her, about must and about must go,
And what the hill's suddenness resists, win so.
Yet strive so, that before age, death's twilight,
Thy soul rest, for none can work in that night.
85 To will implies delay; therefore now do.
Hard deeds, the body's pains; hard knowledge too,
The mind's endeavors reach; and mysteries
Are like the sun, dazzling, yet plain to all eyes.
Keep the truth which thou hast found; men do not stand
90 In so ill case here that God hath with his hand
Signed kings blank charters to kill whom they hate,
Nor are they vicars, but hangmen to fate.
Fool and wretch, wilt thou let thy soul be tied
To man's laws, by which she shall not be tried
95 At the last day? Oh, will it then boot thee
To say a Philip or a Gregory,
A Harry or a Martin taught thee this?
Is not this excuse for mere contraries
Equally strong? Cannot both sides say so?

70 **of force** necessarily   75 **none** *i.e.,* no religion   76 **image**
(the veneration of images was disputed between the Roman
and Protestant churches)   77 **way** road   82 **suddenness** steep-
ness   92 **vicars** proxies (for God)   95 **boot** avail   96 **Philip**
Philip II, king of Spain   **Gregory** one of the popes of that
name   97 **Harry** King Henry VIII   **Martin** Luther   98 **mere**
absolute

That thou mayst rightly obey power, her bounds know;   100
Those passed, her nature, and name is changed; to be
Then humble to her is idolatry.
As streams are, power is; those blest flowers that dwell
At the rough stream's calm head thrive and do well,
But having left their roots and themselves given   105
To the stream's tyrannous rage, alas, are driven
Through mills and rocks and woods, and at last, almost
Consumed in going, in the sea are lost.
So perish souls which more choose men's unjust
Power from God claimed than God himself to trust.   110

LETTERS TO SEVERAL PERSONAGES

※

The Storm

TO MR. CHRISTOPHER BROOKE

Thou which art I ('tis nothing to be so),
Thou which art still thyself, by these shalt know
Part of our passage; and a hand or eye
By Hilliard drawn is worth an history
5 By a worse painter made; and (without pride)
When by thy judgment they are dignified,
My lines are such. 'Tis the pre-eminence
Of friendship only to impute excellence.

England, to whom we owe what we be and have,
10 Sad that her sons did seek a foreign grave
(For fate's or fortune's drifts none can soothsay;
Honor and misery have one face and way),
From out her pregnant entrails sighed a wind
Which at the air's middle marble room did find
15 Such strong resistance that itself it threw
Downward again, and so when it did view
How in the port our fleet dear time did leese,
Withering like prisoners which lie but for fees,
Mildly it kissed our sails, and fresh and sweet,
20 As to a stomach starved, whose insides meet,

The Storm this poem (like the next) describes an incident of
the naval expedition to the Azores in the summer of 1597 for
the purpose of capturing the Spanish silver fleet from America
Christopher Brooke a fellow-student at Lincoln's Inn and sub-
sequently the best man at Donne's wedding 2 **these** *i.e.*, this
letter 3 **passage** voyage 4 **Hilliard** Nicholas Hilliard (1537-
1619), a portrait painter **history** a picture of a series of
events 11 **drifts** purposes **soothsay** predict 14 **middle mar-
ble room** the frozen middle region of the air, supposed to drive
back winds which mounted to it 17 **leese** lose 18 **fees** *i.e.*,
those which must be paid to the jailer before release

70

Meat comes, it came and swole our sails, when we
So joyed as Sarah her swelling joyed to see.
But 'twas but so kind as our countrymen
Which bring friends one day's way and leave them then.
Then, like two mighty kings which, dwelling far   25
Asunder, meet against a third to war,
The south and west winds joined, and as they blew,
Waves like a rolling trench before them threw.
Sooner than you read this line, did the gale,
Like shot not feared till felt, our sails assail,   30
And what at first was called a gust, the same
Hath now a storm's, anon a tempest's name.
Jonas, I pity thee, and curse those men
Who when the storm raged most, did wake thee then;
Sleep is pain's easiest salve, and doth fulfill   35
All offices of death except to kill.
But when I waked, I saw that I saw not.
Ay, and the sun which should teach me had forgot
East, west, day, night; and I could only say
If the world had lasted, now it had been day.   40
Thousands our noises were; yet we 'mongst all
Could none by his right name, but thunder, call.
Lightning was all our light, and it rained more
Than if the sun had drunk the sea before.
Some coffined in their cabins lie, equally   45
Grieved that they are not dead and yet must die;
And as sin-burdened souls from graves will creep
At the last day, some forth their cabins peep
And tremblingly ask what news, and do hear so,
Like jealous husbands, what they would not know.   50
Some, sitting on the hatches, would seem there
With hideous gazing to fear away fear.
Then note they the ship's sicknesses, the mast
Shaked with his ague, and the hold and waist
With a salt dropsy clogged, and all our tacklings   55
Snapping like too high-stretchèd treble strings.
And from our tattered sails rags drop down so

21 **swole** swelled **when** and then 22 **Sarah** the wife of Abra-
ham who, at the age of 80 or thereabouts, bore him a son
(Genesis xxi) 33 **Jonas** *i.e.,* Jonah (see Jonah i. 6) 35 **fulfill**
perform 48 **last day** *i.e.,* the day of judgment 55 **salt dropsy**
i.e., sea water

As from one hanged in chains a year ago.
Even our ordnance, placed for our defense,
60 Strivė to break loose and 'scape away from thence.
Pumping hath tired our men, and what's the gain?
Seas into seas thrown we suck in again;
Hearing hath deafed our sailors, and if they
Knew how to hear, there's none knows what to say.
65 Compared to these storms, death is but a qualm,
Hell somewhat lightsome, and the Bermudas calm.
Darkness, light's elder brother, his birthright
Claims o'er this world, and to heaven hath chased light.
All things are one, and that one none can be,
70 Since all forms, uniform deformity
Doth cover so that we, except God say
Another *fiat*, shall have no more day.
So violent, yet long, these furies be
That though thine absence starve me, I wish not thee.

The Calm

Our storm is past, and that storm's tyrannous rage
A stupid calm (but nothing it) doth 'suage.
The fable is inverted, and far more
A block afflicts now than a stork before.
5 Storms chafe, and soon wear out themselves or us;
In calms heaven laughs to see us languish thus.
As steady as I can wish that my thoughts were,
Smooth as thy mistress' glass or what shines there,
The sea is now. And as the isles which we
10 Seek when we can move, our ships rooted be.
As water did in storms, now pitch runs out
As lead when a fired church becomes one spout.
And all our beauty and our trim decays
Like courts removing or like ended plays.

65 **qualm** fainting fit 66 **the Bermudas** (reputedly stormy)
67 **elder brother** (darkness preceded the creation) 70 **forms**
visible things (objects of cover) 72 *fiat* God's command at
the creation (Genesis i. 3) 3 **fable** (in Æsop's fable King
Stork afflicts the frogs more than King Log) 11 **runs out**
(from the seams of the ship) 12 **lead** (with which the roof
is covered)

The fighting place now seamen's rags supply,   15
And all the tackling is a frippery.
No use of lanterns; and in one place lay
Feathers and dust, today and yesterday.
Earth's hollownesses, which the world's lungs are,
Have no more wind than the upper vault of air.   20
We can nor lost friends nor sought foes recover,
But meteor-like, save that we move not, hover.
Only the calenture together draws
Dear friends, which meet dead in great fishes' jaws.
And on the hatches as on altars lies   25
Each one, his own priest and own sacrifice.
Who live, that miracle do multiply
Where walkers in hot ovens do not die.
If in despite of these we swim, that hath
No more refreshing than our brimstone bath,   30
But from the sea into the ship we turn
Like parboiled wretches on the coals to burn.
Like Bajazet encaged, the shepherd's scoff,
Or like slack-sinewed Samson, his hair off,
Languish our ships. Now, as a myriad   35
Of ants durst the emperor's loved snake invade,
The crawling galleys, sea jails, finny chips,
Might brave our Venices, now bedrid ships.
Whether a rotten state and hope of gain,
Or to disuse me from the queasy pain   40
Of being beloved and loving, or the thirst
Of honor or fair death out-pushed me first,
I lose my end, for here as well as I
A desperate may live and a coward die.

15 **supply** fill up   16 **frippery** second-hand clothing shop   21
left friends *i.e.,* the other ships of the fleet   23 **calenture** a
delirium which impels its victims to jump overboard   27 **Who
live** those who live   28 **walkers** the Jews whom Nebuchadnez-
zar cast into a fiery furnace (Daniel iii)   33 **Bajazet** the Turkish
emperor captured and kept in a cage by Tamburlaine
(**the shepherd**)   36 **snake** the pet snake belonging to the
emperor Tiberius which was devoured by ants   37 **jails** (gal-
leys were usually rowed by prisoners)   **finny chips** *i.e.,* the
galleys, which are as small as chips and are propelled by fins
(oars)   38 **Venices** ships, so called (presumably) because
surrounded by water

45   Stag, dog, and all which from or towards flies
        Is paid with life or prey, or doing dies.
        Fate grudges us all, and doth subtly lay
        A scourge 'gainst which we all forget to pray;
        He that at sea prays for more wind, as well
50   Under the poles may beg cold, heat in hell.
        What are we then? How little more, alas,
        Is man now than before he was! He was
        Nothing; for us, we are for nothing fit;
        Chance or ourselves still disproportion it.
55   We have no power, no will, no sense—I lie!
        I should not then thus feel this misery.

To Sir Henry Wotton from Court

Here's no more news than virtue. I may as well
Tell you Cales' or Saint Michael's tale for news as tell
That vice doth here habitually dwell.

Yet, as to get stomachs we walk up and down
5   And toil to sweeten rest, so may God frown
If but to loathe both I haunt court or town.

For here no one is from the extremity
Of vice by any other reason free
But that the next to him still is worse than he.

10   In this world's warfare they whom rugged fate,
God's commissary, doth so throughly hate
As in the court's squadron to marshal their state,

If they stand armed with silly honesty,
With wishing prayers and neat integrity,
15   Like Indians 'gainst Spanish hosts they be.

Suspicious boldness to this place belongs,
And to have as many ears as all have tongues,

53 **for us** as for us 2 **Cales'** Cadiz' (see "Principal Dates,"
p. xvii, 1596) **St. Michael's** in the Azores (idem, 1597) **4
stomachs** appetites **11 commissary** deputy **throughly** thoroughly **13 silly** simple

Tender to know, tough to acknowledge wrongs.

Believe me, sir, in my youth's giddiest days,
When to be like the court was a play's praise,   20
Plays were not so like courts as courts are like plays.

Then let us at these mimic antics jest,
Whose deepest projects and egregious gests
Are but dull morals of a game at chests.

But now 'tis incongruity to smile.   25
Therefore I end, and bid farewell awhile—
At court, though *from court* were the better style.

To Sir Henry Wotton at his Going Ambassador to Venice

After those reverend papers whose soul is
    Our good and great king's loved hand and feared name,
By which to you he derives much of his,
    And (how he may) makes you almost the same—

A taper of his torch, a copy writ   5
    From his original, and a fair beam
Of the same warm and dazzling sun, though it
    Must in another sphere his virtue stream;

After those learned papers which your hand
    Hath stored with notes of use and pleasure too,   10
From which rich treasury you may command
    Fit matter, whether you will write or do;

After those loving papers where friends send
    With glad grief to your seaward steps, farewell,
Which thicken on you now, as prayers ascend   15
    To heaven in troops at a good man's passing bell;

22 **antics** mountebanks 23 **gests** exploits 24 **morals** symbols
chests chess 27 *from* away from 1 **papers** *i.e.,* Wotton's
commission from the king 3 **derives** imparts 8 **his** *i.e.,* the
beam's **virtue** efficacy **stream** emit

Admit this honest paper and allow
    It such an audience as yourself would ask.
What you must say at Venice, this means now,
20   And hath for nature what you have for task

To swear much love—not to be changed before
    Honor alone will to your fortune fit;
Nor shall I then honor your fortune more
    Than I have done your noble wanting it.

25 But 'tis an easier load, though both oppress,
    To want than govern greatness, for we are
In that our own and only business;
    In this we must for others' vices care.

'Tis therefore well your spirits now are placed
30   In their last furnace, in activity,
Which fits them (schools and courts and wars o'erpassed)
    To touch and test in any best degree.

For me (if there be such a thing as I)
    Fortune (if there be such a thing as she)
35 Spies that I bear so well her tyranny
    That she thinks nothing else so fit for me.

But though she part us, to hear my oft prayers
    For your increase God is as near me here,
And to send you what I shall beg, his stairs
40   In length and ease are alike everywhere.

To the Countess of Bedford

Madam,
Reason is our soul's left hand, faith her right;
    By these we reach divinity—that's you.
Their loves, who have the blessings of your sight,

22 **Honor . . . fit** fortune raises you so far above me that
I must honor rather than love you 26 **want** lack 27 **that** i.e.,
lack of greatness 28 **this** i.e., the government of greatness
care be careful 31 **schools . . . wars** (in all of which Wotton
had distinguished himself) 32 **touch** try

Grew from their reason; mine from fair faith grew.

But as, although a squint left-handedness   5
    Be ungracious, yet we cannot want that hand,
So would I (not to increase, but to express
    My faith) as I believe, so understand.

Therefore I study you first in your saints,
    Those friends whom your election glorifies,   10
Then in your deeds, accesses, and restraints,
    And what you read, and what yourself devise.

But soon the reasons why you are loved by all
    Grow infinite, and so pass reason's reach;
Then back again to implicit faith I fall,   15
    And rest on what the catholic voice doth teach:

That you are good. And not one heretic
    Denies it; if he did, yet you are so,
For rocks which, high to sense, deep-rooted stick,
    Waves wash, not undermine nor overthrow.   20

In everything there naturally grows
    A balsamum to keep it fresh and new,
If 'twere not injured by extrinsic blows;
    Your birth and beauty are this balm in you.

But you of learning and religión   25
    And virtue and such ingredients have made
A mithridate whose operatión
    Keeps off or cures what can be done or said.

Yet this is not your physic, but your food,
    A diet fit for you, for you are here   30
The first good angel, since the world's frame stood,
    That ever did in woman's shape appear.

---

5 **squint** oblique   6 **want** do without   11 **accesses** approaches,
i.e., steps taken   16 **catholic** general   18 **yet** nevertheless
19 **sense** sight   22 **balsamum** the moisture inherent in all living
things, supposed to impart vitality to them   27 **mithridate**
antidote   29 **physic** medicine

Since you are then God's masterpiece, and so
His factor for our loves, do as you do;
35 Make your return home gracious, and bestow
This life on that; so make one life of two.
For so God help me, I would not miss you there
For all the good which you can do me here.

To the Countess of Huntingdon

Madam,
Man to God's image, Eve to man's was made,
Nor find we that God breathed a soul in her;
Canons will not church functions you invade,
Nor laws to civil office you prefer.

5 Who vagrant, transitory comets sees,
Wonders because they are rare; but a new star
Whose motion with the firmament agrees
Is miracle, for there no new things are.

In woman so perchance mild innocence
10 A seldom comet is, but active good
A miracle which reason 'scapes, and sense,
For art and nature this in them withstood.

As such a star the Magi led to view
The manger-cradled infant, God below,
15 By virtue's beams (by fame derived from you)
May apt souls, and the worst may, virtue know.

If the world's age and death be argued well
By the sun's fall, which now towards earth doth bend,

34 factor purchasing agent   **35 home** i.e., heaven   **36 that** i.e.,
the life to come   **37 there** i.e., in the next world   **1 to** accord-
ing to, in   **2 find we** can we learn   **3 Canons** laws of the
church will not . . . **you** i.e., forbid you to   **7 firmament** the
sphere of the fixed stars in the heavens   **8 there** i.e., in the
firmament, conceived as unchangeable   **12 them** i.e., women
withstood opposed   **15 by fame** according to report   **17-18
argued well By** correctly inferred from   **18 sun's fall** (pre-
sumably) its altered position in the Copernican astronomy

Then we might fear that virtue, since she fell
   So low as woman, should be near her end.   20

But she's not stooped, but raised; exiled by men
   She fled to heaven, that's heavenly things, that's you;
She was in all men thinly scattered then,
   But now amassed, contracted in a few.

She gilded us, but you are gold and she;   25
   Us she informed, but transubstantiates you;
Soft dispositións which ductile be,
   Elixir-like, she makes not clean, but new.

Though you a wife's and mother's name retain,
   'Tis not as woman, for all are not so;   30
But virtue, having made you virtue, is fain
   To adhere in these names, her and you to show;

Else, being alike pure, we should neither see;
   As water being into air rarefied,
Neither appear till in one cloud they be,   35
   So for our sakes you do low names abide;

Taught by great constellations (which being framed
   Of the most stars, take low names, Crab and Bull,
When single planets by the gods are named),
   You covet not great names, of great things full.   40

So you as woman, one doth comprehend,
   And in the veil of kindred others see;
To some ye are revealed as in a friend,
   And as a virtuous prince far off, to me.

To whom, because from you all virtues flow,   45
   And 'tis not none to dare contémplate you,
I, which do so, as your true subject owe

22 **that's** that means   23 **then** in former times   26 **informed** imbued **transubstantiates** changes (into virtue itself)   28 **Elixirlike** like the elixir vitæ, which cures all diseases and prolongs life   30 **all** *i.e.*, all women   31 **is fain** would like to   33 **neither** *i.e.*, neither virtue nor you   38 **most** greatest   39 **by** after   41 **one** *i.e.*, her husband   46 **none** *i.e.*, no virtue

Some tribute for that; so these lines are due.

If you can think these flatteries, they are,
50   For then your judgment is below my praise;
If they were so, oft flatteries work as far
    As counsels, and as far the endeavor raise.

So my ill, reaching you, might there grow good,
    But I remain a poisoned fountain still;
55 But not your beauty, virtue, knowledge, blood
    Are more above all flattery than my will.

And if I flatter any. 'tis not you,
    But my own judgment, who did long ago
Pronounce that all these praises should be true,
60   And virtue should your beauty and birth outgrow.

Now that my prophecies are all fulfilled,
    Rather than God should not be honored too
And all these gifts confessed which he instilled,
    Yourself were bound to say that which I do.

65 So I but your recorder am in this,
    Or mouth, or speaker of the universe,
A ministerial notary, for 'tis
    Not I, but you and fame that make this verse.

I was your prophet in your younger days,
70 And now your chaplain, God in you to praise.

53 **ill** *i.e.,* flattery   67 **ministerial** instrument   **notary secretary**

EPICEDES AND OBSEQUIES

❧

Elegy on the Lady Markham

Man is the world, and death the oceán
To which God gives the lower parts of man.
This sea environs all, and though as yet
God hath set marks and bounds 'twixt us and it,
Yet doth it roar and gnaw and still pretend,   5
And breaks our banks whene'er it takes a friend.
Then our land waters (tears of passion) vent;
Our waters, then, above our firmament
(Tears which our soul doth for her sins let fall)
Take all a brackish taste and funeral,   10
And even these tears which should wash sin are sin.
We, after God's *no,* drown our world again.
Nothing but man, of all envenomed things,
Doth work upon itself with inborn stings.
Tears are false spectacles; we cannot see   15
Through passion's mist what we are, or what she.
In her this sea of death hath made no breach,
But as the tide doth wash the slimy beach
And leaves embroidered works upon the sand,
So is her flesh refined by death's cold hand.   20
As men of China after an age's stay
Do take up porcelain where they buried clay,
So at this grave (her limbec, which refines
The diamonds, rubies, sapphires, pearls, and mines

5 **pretend** extend (its bounds)   7 **vent** flow   8 (the waters
above the firmament (Genesis i 7) were usually understood
as the moisture in the upper air which was precipitated as
rain)   12 **no** *i.e.,* God's promise not to destroy the world again
by flood (Genesis ix. 11)   **our world** *i.e.,* the microcosm, man
22 **clay** (porcelain was believed to be clay which had been
buried underground a hundred years)   23 **limbec** retort used
in distillation   24 **mines** precious metals

81

25   Of which this flesh was) her soul shall inspire
        Flesh of such stuff as God, when his last fire
        Annuls this world, to recompense it, shall
        Make and name then the elixir of this all.
        They say the sea, when it gains, loseth too;
30   If carnal death (the younger brother) do
        Usurp the body, our soul, which subject is
        To the elder death by sin, is freed by this.
        They perish both when they attempt the just,
        For graves our trophies are and both deaths' dust.
35   So, unobnoxious now, she hath buried both,
        For none to death sins that to sin is loath,
        Nor do they die which are not loath to die;
        So hath she this and that virginity.
        Grace was in her extremely diligent,
40   That kept her from sin, yet made her repent.
        Of what small spots pure white complains! Alas,
        How little poison cracks a crystal glass!
        She sinned but just enough to let us see
        That God's word must be true: "All sinners be."
45   So much did zeal her conscience rarefy
        That éxtreme truth lacked little of a lie,
        Making omissions acts, laying the touch
        Of sin on things that sometimes may be such.
        As Moses' cherubins, whose natures do
50   Surpass all speed, by him are winged too,
        So would her soul, already in heaven, seem then
        To climb by tears, the common stairs of men.
        How fit she was for God I am content
        To speak, that death his vain haste may repent.
55   How fit for us, how even and how sweet,
        How good in all her titles, and how meet
        To have reformed this forward heresy,
        That women can no parts of friendship be,

25 **inspire** breathe into   28 **elixir** an essence (the elixir of life)
supposed to prolong life indefinitely   **all** the universe (object of
make and **name**)   29 **when it gains, loseth too** *i.e.*, eats away
the shore in some places and piles up sand in others   33 **at-
tempt** try to injure   34 **both deaths' dust** *i.e.*, it is not we but
sin and the death of the body that are buried   35 **unobnoxious**
invulnerable   38 **this and that virginity** victory over sin and
victory over death   57 **forward** presumptuous

How moral, how divine, shall not be told,
Lest they that hear her virtues think her old,
And lest we take death's part and make him glad
Of such a prey, and to his triumph add.

Of the Progress of the Soul

WHEREIN, BY OCCASION OF THE RELIGIOUS DEATH OF
MISTRESS ELIZABETH DRURY, THE INCOMMODITIES OF THE
SOUL IN THIS LIFE AND HER EXALTATION IN THE NEXT
ARE CONTEMPLATED

The Second Anniversary

The
en-
trance.

Nothing could make me sooner to confess
That this world had an everlastingness,
Than to consider that a year is run
Since both this lower world's and the sun's Sun,
5 The luster and the vigor of this all,
Did set—'twere blasphemy to say, "did fall."
But as a ship which hath strook sail doth run
By force of that force which before it won,
Or as sometimes in a beheaded man,
10 Though at those two Red Seas which freely ran,
One from the trunk, another from the head,
His soul be sailed to her eternal bed,
His eyes will twinkle and his tongue will roll
As though he beckoned and called back his soul,
15 He grasps his hands, and he pulls up his feet,
And seems to reach, and to step forth to meet
His soul (when all these motions which we saw
Are but as ice which crackles at a thaw),
Or as a lute which in moist weather rings
20 Her knell alone by cracking of her strings:
So struggles this dead world now she is gone,
For there is motion in corruption.
As some days are at the creation named
Before the sun, the which framed days, was framed,
25 So after this Sun's set some show appears,
And orderly vicissitude of years.

marginal note **entrance** beginning   **5 this all** the universe   **23
named** (according to the account in Genesis, the sun was **not**
created till the fourth day)   **24 the which framed** which de-
fined, measured   **26 vicissitude** natural progress

Yet a new deluge, and of Lethe flood,
Hath drowned us all: all have forgot all good,
Forgetting her, the main reserve of all.
Yet in this deluge, gross and general,   30
Thou seest me strive for life. My life shall be
To be hereafter praised for praising thee,
Immortal maid, who, though thou wouldst refuse
The name of mother, be unto my muse
A father, since her chaste ambition is   35
Yearly to bring forth such a child as this.
These hymns may work on future wits, and so
May great-grandchildren of thy praises grow,
And so, though not revive, embalm and spice
The world, which else would putrefy with vice;   40
For thus man may extend thy progeny
Until man do but vanish, and not die.
These hymns thy issue may increase so long
As till God's great *Venite* change the song.
Thirst for that time, O my insatiate soul,   A just
And serve thy thirst with God's safe-sealing bowl.   disesti-
Be thirsty still and drink still till thou go   mation
To the only health, to be hydroptic so.   of this
Forget this rotten world, and unto thee   world.
Let thine own times as an old story be.   50
Be not concerned. Study not why nor when;
Do not so much as not believe a man,
For though to err be worst, to try truths forth ·
Is far more business than this world is worth.
The world is but a carcass; thou art fed   55
By it but as a worm that carcass bred.
And why shouldst thou, poor worm, consider more
When this world will grow better than before,
Than those thy fellow-worms do think upon
That carcass's last resurrectión?   60
Forget this world, and scarce think of it so
As of old clothes cast off a year ago.
To be thus stupid is alacrity;

27 **Lethe flood** water from the river in Hades which produces
forgetfulness   38 **grow** raise up   44 *Venite* the summons to
the day of judgment   46 **safe-sealing bowl** *i.e.*, the eucharist
47 **still** ever   48 **hydroptic** thirsty, (literally) dropsical   53
try . . . forth put to the proof   63 **stupid** dull, slow

Men thus lethargic have best memory.

65 Look upward; that's towards her whose happy state
We now lament not, but congratulate.
She to whom all this world was but a stage
Where all sat heark'ning how her youthful age
Should be employed, because in all she did

70 Some figure of the golden times was hid,
Who could not lack whate'er this world could give,
Because she was the form that made it live,
Nor could complain that this world was unfit
To be stayed in then when she was in it,

75 She that first tried indifferent desires
By virtue, and virtue by religious fires,
She to whose person paradise adhered
As courts to princes, she whose eyes ensphered
Starlight enough to have made the south control

80 (Had she been there) the star-full northern pole,
She, she is gone. She is gone. When thou know'st this,
What fragmentary rubbish this world is
Thou know'st, and that it is not worth a thought;
He honors it too much that thinks it nought.

85 Think then, my soul, that death is but a groom
Which brings a taper to the outward room,
Whence thou spiest first a little, glimmering light,
And after brings it nearer to thy sight;
For such approaches doth heaven make in death.
Think thyself laboring now with broken breath,
And think those broken and soft notes to be
Division and thy happiest harmony.
Think thee laid on thy deathbed, loose and slack,
And think that but unbinding of a pack

95 To take one precious thing, thy soul, from thence.
Think thyself parched with fever's violence;
Anger thine ague more by calling it

Contem-plation of our state in our death-bed. (side note, lines 86–93)

70 **figure** image, type **golden times** the world in its pristine
purity 72 **form** essence, soul 75 **tried** tested **indifferent**
neutral, not necessarily good or bad 78 **As courts to princes**
(the court is wherever the prince is) 79 **control** overpower,
i.e., outshine 80 **star-full** (the stars which cluster about the
north pole are more numerous than those about the south)
91 **notes** *i.e.,* the feeble and irregular breathing of a dying man
92 **Division** melody

Thy physic; chide the slackness of the fit.
Think that thou hear'st thy knell, and think no more
But that as bells called thee to church before,   100
So this to the triumphant church calls thee.
Think Satan's sergeants round about thee be,
And think that but for legacies they thrust;
Give one thy pride, to another give thy lust;
Give them those sins which they gave thee before,   105
And trust the immaculate blood to wash thy score.
Think thy friends weeping round, and think that they
Weep but because they go not yet thy way.
Think that they close thine eyes, and think in this,
That they confess much in the world amiss,   110
Who dare not trust a dead man's eye with that
Which they from God and angels cover not.
Think that they shroud thee up, and think from thence
They reinvest thee in white innocence.
Think that thy body rots, and (if so low,   115
Thy soul exalted so, thy thoughts can go)
Think thee a prince, who of themselves create
Worms which insensibly devour their state.
Think that they bury thee, and think that rite
Lays thee to sleep but a Saint Lucy's night.   120
Think these things cheerfully, and if thou be
Drowsy or slack, remember then that she,
She whose complexion was so even made
That which of her ingredients should invade
The other three no fear, no art could guess   125
(So far were all removed from more or less;
But as in mithridate or just perfumes
Where, all good things being met, no one presumes
To govern or to triumph on the rest,
Only because all were, no part was best,   130
And as, though all do know that quantities

98 **physic** medicine   **fit** *i.e.*, attack of fever   102 **sergeants** constables   103 **legacies** deathbed bequests   106 **wash** wash out **score** debts   117 **create** (literally) confer offices and honors upon   120 **Saint Lucy's night** the longest night in the year (but still only one night)   123 **complexion** temperament, thought of as a combination of humors (ingredients)   124 **invade** encroach upon   127 **mithridate** antidote against poison   **just** properly mixed   130 **all were** *i.e.*, all were best

Are made of lines, and lines from points arise,
None can these lines or quantities unjoint
And say this is a line, or this a point,
135 So, though the elements and humors were
In her, one could not say, "This governs there");
Whose even constitution might have won
Any disease to venture on the sun
Rather than her, and make a spirit fear
140 That he to disuniting subject were;
To whose proportions if we would compare
Cubes, they are unstable, circles angular,
She who was such a chain as fate employs
To bring mankind all fortunes it enjoys,
145 So fast, so even wrought, as one would think
No accident could threaten any link;
She, she embraced a sickness, gave it meat,
The purest blood and breath that e'er it eat,
And hath taught us that though a good man hath
150 Title to heaven, and plead it by his faith,
And though he may pretend a conquest (since
Heaven was content to suffer violence),
Yea, though he plead a long possession too
(For they're in heaven on earth who heaven's works do),
155 Though he had right and power and place before,
Yet death must usher, and unlock the door.
Think further on thyself, my soul, and think
How thou at first wast made but in a sink;
Think that it argued some infirmity
160 That those two souls which then thou found'st in me
Thou fed'st upon and drew'st into thee, both
My second soul of sense and first of growth.
Think but how poor thou wast, how obnoxíous,

133 **unjoint** separate 135 **elements** prime matter (air, **fire,**
earth, water) **humors** the fluids of the human body 137
even (therefore incorruptible) **won** prevailed upon 138 **sun**
(which is immune to disease) 140 **disuniting** (a spirit is im-
material and therefore not subject to disuniting) 151 **pretend**
lay claim to 152 **violence** "And from the days of John the
Baptist until now the kingdom of heaven suffereth violence"
(Matthew xi. 12) 160 **thou** i.e., the rational soul 162 **sec-
ond** . . . **first** (according to the threefold division of the facul-
ties of the soul—growth, feeling, reason) 163 **obnoxious** liable
to injury

Whom a small lump of flesh could poison thus.
This curded milk, this poor unlittered whelp,   165
My body, could, beyond escape or help,
Infect thee with original sin, and thou
Couldst neither then refuse, nor leave it now.
Think that no stubborn, sullen anchorite
Which, fixed to a pillar or a grave, doth sit   170
Bedded and bathed in all his ordures, dwells
So foully as our souls in their first-built cells.
Think in how poor a prison thou didst lie
After, enabled but to suck and cry.
Think, when 'twas grown to most, 'twas a poor inn,   175
A province packed up in two yards of skin,
And that usurped or threatened with the rage
Of sicknesses or their true mother, age.
But think that death hath now enfranchised thee;
Thou hast thy expansion now, and liberty.   180
Think that a rusty piece, discharged, is flown
In pieces, and the bullet is his own
And freely flies. This to thy soul allow:
Think thy shell broke, think thy soul hatched but now,
And think this slow-paced soul, which late did cleave   185
To a body, and went but by the body's leave,
Twenty, perchance, or thirty mile a day,
Dispatches in a minute all the way
'Twixt heaven and earth. She stays not in the air
To look what meteors there themselves prepare;   190
She carries no desire to know, nor sense,
Whether the air's middle region be intense;
For the element of fire, she doth not know
Whether she passed by such a place or no;
She baits not at the moon, nor cares to try   195
Whether in that new world men live and die.
Venus retards her not to inquire how she
Can, being one star, Hesper and Vesper be.

169 **anchorite** hermit   175 **to most** to the full   181 **flown** split
182 **his own** *i.e.*, at liberty   190 **meteors** atmospheric phe-
nomena (wind, rain, the rainbow, lightning, etc.)   192 **mid-
dle region** the middle part of the ring of air between the earth
and the moon   **intense** turbulent   193 **fire** the disputed region
of fire just beneath the moon   195 **baits** stops (for refresh-
ment)   198 **Hesper** the morning star (according to Donne)
Vesper the evening star

He that charmed Argus' eyes, sweet Mercury,
200 Works not on her, who now is grown all eye,
Who, if she meet the body of the sun,
Goes through, not staying till his course be run,
Who finds in Mars his camp no corps of guard,
Nor is by Jove nor by his father barred,
205 But ere she can consider how she went,
At once is at, and through the firmament.
And as these stars were but so many beads
Strung on one string, speed undistinguished leads
Her through those spheres as through the beads a string
210 Whose quick succession makes it still one thing.
As doth the pith, which, lest our bodies slack,
Strings fast the little bones of neck and back,
So by the soul doth death string heaven and earth,
For when our soul enjoys this her third birth
215 (Creation gave her one, a second, grace),
Heaven is as near and present to her face
As colors are, and objects, in a room
Where darkness was before, when tapers come.
This must, my soul, thy long-short progress be.
220 To advance these thoughts remember then that she,
She, whose fair body no such prison was
But that a soul might well be pleased to pass
An age in her, she whose rich beauty lent
Mintage to other beauties, for they went
225 But for so much as they were like to her,
She, in whose body (if we dare prefer
This low world to so high a mark as she)
The western treasure, eastern spicery,
Europe and Afric and the unknown rest
230 Were easily found, or what in them was best
(And when we have made this large discovery
Of all in her some one part then will be
Twenty such parts, whose plenty and riches is
Enough to make twenty such worlds as this),

199 **charmed** *i.e.*, put to sleep (Argus had a hundred eyes)
203 **Mars his** Mars'   **corps of guard** guard, guardhouse 204
Jove the planet Jupiter **his father** Saturn 206 **firmament**
sphere of the fixed stars 207 **as** as if 208 **undistinguished**
(presumably) too swift to be discerned or measured 211
pith spinal cord 224 **Mintage** currency, value

She, whom had they known, who did first betroth   235
The tutelar angels, and assigned one both
To nations, cities, and to companies,
To functions, offices, and dignities,
And to each several man, to him, and him,
They would have given her one for every limb,   240
She, of whose soul, if we may say 'twas gold,
Her body was the electrum, and did hold
Many degrees of that (we understood
Her by her sight; her pure and eloquent blood
Spoke in her cheeks, and so distinctly wrought   245
That one might almost say her body thought),
She, she, thus richly and largely housed, is gone,
And chides us slow-paced snails who crawl upon
Our prison's prison, earth, nor think us well
Longer than whilst we bear our brittle shell.   250
But 'twere but little to have changed our room
If, as we were in this our living tomb
Oppressed with ignorance, we still were so.
Poor soul, in this thy flesh what dost thou know?
Thou know'st thyself so little, as thou know'st not
How thou didst die nor how thou wast begot.
Thou neither know'st how thou at first cam'st in
Nor how thou took'st the poison of man's sin.
Nor dost thou (though thou know'st that thou art so)
By what way thou art made immortal know.   260
Thou art too narrow, wretch, to comprehend
Even thyself, yea, though thou wouldst but bend
To know thy body. Have not all souls thought
For many ages that our body is wrought
Of air and fire and other elements?   265
And now they think of new ingredients,
And one soul thinks one, and another way
Another thinks, and 'tis an even lay.
Know'st thou but how the stone doth enter in

*Her ig-
norance
in this
life and
knowl-
edge in
the next.*

235 **they** those 236 **tutelar** guardian 239 **several** indi-
vidual 242 **electrum** alloy of gold and silver 243 **that** *i.e.*,
gold, *i.e.*, the soul 244 **sight** appearance 251 **room** place
255 as that 262 **bend** (1) stoop, (2) address oneself 266
new ingredients (Paracelsus (d. 1541) argued that the body is
composed of salt, sulphur, and mercury rather than the usual
four elements) 268 **lay** bet

270 The bladder's cave and never break the skin?
Know'st thou how blood which to the heart doth flow
Doth from one ventricle to the other go?
And for the putrid stuff which thou dost spit,
Know'st thou how thy lungs have attracted it?
275 There are no passages; so that there is
(For ought thou know'st) piercing of substances.
And of those many opinions which men raise
Of nails and hairs, dost thou know which to praise?
What hope have we to know ourselves, when we
280 Know not the least things which for our use be?
We see in authors, too stiff to recant,
A hundred controversies of an ant,
And yet one watches, starves, freezes, and sweats
To know but catechisms and alphabets
285 Of unconcerning things, matters of fact:
How others on our stage their parts did act,
What Caesar did, yea, and what Cicero said.
Why grass is green, or why our blood is red
Are mysteries which none have reached unto.
290 In this low form, poor soul, what wilt thou do?
When wilt thou shake off this pedantery
Of being taught by sense and fantasy?
Thou look'st through spectacles; small things seem great
Below; but up unto the watch-tower get,
295 And see all things despoiled of fallacies.
Thou shalt not peep through lattices of eyes,
Nor hear through labyrinths of ears, nor learn
By circuit or collections to discern.
In heaven thou straight know'st all concerning it,
300 And what concerns it not, shalt straight forget.
There thou (but in no other school) mayst be,
Perchance, as learned and as full as she,
She who all libraries had throughly read
At home in her own thoughts, and practisèd

278 **nails and hairs** (whether they were parts of the body was
disputed) **praise** value, prize 281 **stiff** obstinate 283
watches goes without sleep 284 **catechisms and alphabets** *i.e.,*
the most elementary knowledge 290 **form** state 292 **sense**
sensation **fantasy** imagination 294 **watch-tower** *i.e.,* heaven
295 **despoiled** stripped 298 **circuit** roundabout reasoning **col-
lections** inferences 303 **throughly** thoroughly

So much good as would make as many more,   305
She whose example they must all implore
Who would or do or think well, and confess
That all the virtuous actions they express
Are but a new and worse edition
Of her some one thought or one action,   310
She who in the art of knowing heaven was grown
Here upon earth to such perfection
That she hath, ever since to heaven she came,
(In a far fairer print) but read the same,
She, she, not satisfied with all this weight   315
(For so much knowledge as would overfreight
Another did but ballast her) is gone
As well to enjoy as get perfection,
And calls us after her in that she took
(Taking herself) our best and worthiest book.   320
Return not, my soul, from this ecstasy   *Of our*
And meditation of what thou shalt be,   *company*
To earthly thoughts till it to thee appear,   *in this*
With whom thy conversation must be there.   *life and*
With whom wilt thou converse? what station   *in the*
Canst thou choose out, free from infection,   *next.*
That will not give thee theirs nor drink in thine?
Shalt thou not find a spongy, slack divine
Drink and suck in the instructions of great men,
And for the word of God vent them again?   330
Are there not some courts (and then, no things be
So 'like as courts) which in this let us see
That wits and tongues of libelers are weak,
Because they do more ill than these can speak?
The poison's gone through all; poisons affect   335
Chiefly the chiefest parts, but some effect
In nails and hairs, yea excrements, will show;
So will the poison of sin in the most low.
Up, up, my drowsy soul, where thy new ear
Shall in the angels' songs no discord hear,   340
Where thou shalt see the blessèd Mother-maid

---

305 **more** *i.e.*, more libraries   307 **or do** either do   321 **ecstasy** state of rapture   325 **station** *i.e.*, station in life   327 **theirs** *i.e.*, their infection   331 **courts** *i.e.*, courts of kings and princes   334 **they** *i.e.*, the courts

Joy in not being that which men have said,
Where she's exalted more for being good
Than for her interest of motherhood.
345 Up to those patriarchs, which did longer sit
Expecting Christ than they have enjoyed him yet.
Up to those prophets, which now gladly see
Their prophecies grown to be history.
Up to the apostles, who did bravely run
350 All the sun's course with more light than the sun.
Up to those martyrs, who did calmly bleed
Oil to the apostles' lamps, dew to their seed.
Up to those virgins, who thought that almost
They made joint-tenants with the Holy Ghost
355 If they to any should His temple give.
Up, up! for in that squadron there doth live
She who hath carried thither new degrees
(As to their number) to their dignities,
She who, being to herself a state, enjoyed
360 All royalties which any state employed,
For she made wars and triumphed; reason still
Did not o'erthrow, but rectify her will;
And she made peace, for no peace is like this,
That beauty and chastity together kiss;
365 She did high justice, for she crucified
Every first motion of rebellious pride;
And she gave pardons and was liberal,
For, only herself except, she pardoned all;
She coined, in this, that her impressions gave
370 To all our actions all the worth they have;
She gave protections: the thoughts of her breast
Satan's rude officers could ne'er arrest.
As these prerogatives, being met in one,
Made her a sovereign state, religión
375 Made her a church, and these two made her all.

342 **that . . . said** *i.e.*, possessed of divine attributes 344
interest share 345 **longer** *i.e.*, during the centuries before
Christ 354 **joint-tenants** *i.e.*, they made any one to whom they
gave their bodies (the temple of the Holy Ghost) joint-tenants
355 **temple** *i.e.*, the body (1 Corinthians iii. 16) 360
royalties royal prerogatives 362 **rectify** refine, purify 369
coined, in this issued coins, in this respect 371 **protections**
writs of immunity from arrest

She who was all this all, and could not fall
To worse by company, for she was still
More antidote than all the world was ill,
She, she doth leave it, and by death survive
All this in heaven, whither who doth not strive   380
The more because she's there, he doth not know
That accidental joys in heaven do grow.
But pause, my soul, and study, ere thou fall
On accidental joys, the essentiál.
Still before accessories do abide   385
A trial, must the principal be tried.

Of essential joy in this life and in the next.

And what essential joy canst thou expect
Here upon earth? what permanent effect
Of transitory causes? Dost thou love
Beauty? (And beauty worthiest is to move.)
Poor cozened coz'ner, *that* she and *that* thou
Which did begin to love are neither now.
You are both fluid, changed since yesterday;
Next day repairs (but ill) last day's decay.
Nor are, although the river keep the name,   395
Yesterday's waters and today's the same.
So flows her face and thine eyes; neither now
That saint nor pilgrim which your loving vow
Concerned remains, but whilst you think you be
Constant, you are hourly in inconstancy.   400
Honor may have pretense unto our love,
Because that God did live so long above
Without this honor and then loved it so
That he at last made creatures to bestow
Honor on him, not that he needed it,   405
But that to his hands man might grow more fit.
But since all honors from inferiors flow
(For they do give it; princes do but show
Whom they would have so honored) and that this
On such opinions and capacities   410
Is built as rise and fall to more and less,
Alas, 'tis but a casual happiness.
Hath ever any man to himself assigned

377 **company** association with others   382 **accidental** non-
essential   383-384 **fall On** have recourse to   85 **Still** always
abide undergo   391 **cozened coz'ner** cheated cheater   392
neither different   401 **pretense** claim   409 **that** since

This or that happiness to arrest his mind
415 But that another man which takes a worse
Thinks him a fool for having ta'en that course?
They who did labor Babel's tower to erect
Might have considered that for that effect
All this whole solid earth could not allow
420 Nor furnish forth materials enow,
And that this center, to raise such a place,
Was far too little to have been the base.
No more affords this world foundatión
To erect true joy, were all the means in one.
425 But as the heathen made them several gods
Of all God's benefits and all his rods
(For as the wine and corn and onions are
Gods unto them, so agues be, and war),
And as, by changing that whole, precious gold
430 To such small copper coins, they lost the old,
And lost their only God, who ever must
Be sought alone, and not in such a thrust,
So much mankind true happiness mistakes:
No joy enjoys that man that many makes.
435 Then, soul, to thy first pitch work up again;
Know that all lines which circles do contain,
For once that they the center touch, do touch
Twice the circumference; and be thou such:
Double on heaven thy thoughts on earth employed.
440 All will not serve. Only who have enjoyed
The sight of God in fullness can think it,
For it is both the object and the wit.
This is essential joy, where neither He
Can suffer diminutión, nor we.
445 'Tis such a full and such a filling good,
Had the angels once looked on him, they had stood.
To fill the place of one of them, or more,

414 **arrest** fix (the mind's) attention on   418 **that effect** *i.e.*,
to "reach unto heaven" (Genesis xi. 4)   420 **enow** (plural of)
enough   421 **center** *i.e.*, the earth   424 **in one** *i.e.*, in one erec-
tion, structure   425 **several** separate   429 **whole** perfect, pure
432 **thrust** crowd   434 **many** *i.e.*, many gods   441 **think** con-
ceive of   **it** *i.e.*, the joy (of the sight of God)   442 **object** the
object of knowledge   **wit** knowledge itself   446 **stood** *i.e.*,
not fallen

She whom we celebrate is gone before,
She, who had here so much essential joy
As no chance could distract, much less destroy, 450
Who with God's presence was acquainted so
(Hearing and speaking to him) as to know
His face in any natural stone or tree
Better than when in images they be,
Who kept by diligent devotión 455
God's image in such reparatión
Within her heart that what decay was grown
Was her first parents' fault, and not her own,
Who, being solicited to any act,
Still heard God pleading his safe precontract, 460
Who by a faithful confidence was here
Betrothed to God, and now is married there,
Whose twilights were more clear than our midday,
Who dreamt devoutlier than most use to pray,
Who, being here filled with grace, yet strove to be 465
Both where more grace and more capacity
At once is given—she to heaven is gone,
Who made this world in some proportión
A heaven, and here became, unto us all,
Joy (as our joys admit) essentiál. 470
But could this low world joys essential touch,
Heaven's accidental joys would pass them much.
How poor and lame must then our casual be?
If thy prince will his subjects to call thee
"My lord," and this do swell thee, thou art than,
By being a greater, grown to be less man.
When no physician of redress can speak,
A joyful, casual violence may break
A dangerous aposteme in thy breast,
And whilst thou joyest in this, the dangerous rest, 480
'The bag, may rise up, and so strangle thee.
Whate'er was casual may ever be.

Of accidental joys in both places.

What should the nature change? or make the same
Certain, which was but casual when it came?
485 All casual joy doth loud and plainly say,
Only by coming, that it can away.
Only in heaven joy's strength is never spent,
And accidental things are permanent.
Joy of a soul's arrival ne'er decays,
490 For that soul ever joys and ever stays;
Joy that their last great consummatión
Approaches in the resurrectión,
When earthly bodies more celestial
Shall be than angels were, for they could fall:
495 This kind of joy doth every day admit
Degrees of growth, but none of losing it.
In this fresh joy 'tis no small part that she,
She, in whose goodness he that names degree
Doth injure her ('tis loss to be called best
500 There where the stuff is not such as the rest),
She, who left such a body as even she
Only in heaven could learn how it can be
Made better, for she rather was two souls,
Or like to full, on-both-sides-written rolls,
505 Where eyes might read upon the outward skin
As strong recórds for God, as minds within;
She, who by making full perfection grow,
Pieces a circle and still keeps it so,
Longed for, and longing for it, to heaven is gone,
510 Where she receives and gives additión.

Con- Here in a place where misdevotion frames
clu- A thousand prayers to saints whose very names
sion. The ancient church knew not, heaven knows not yet,
And where what laws of poetry admit,
515 Laws of religion have at least the same,
Immortal maid, I might invoke thy name.
Could any saint provoke that appetite,
Thou here shouldst make me a French convertite,

486 can can go 499 loss detriment 505 outward skin right
side of a parchment 508 Pieces completes so i.e., perfectly
circular 510 addition honors 511 place i.e., France 514
what . . . admit i.e., the invocation of the muse 515 the
same i.e., the same things admitted it

But thou wouldst not, nor wouldst thou be content
To take this for my second year's true rent, 520
Did this coin bear any other stamp than His
That gave thee power to do, me to say this.
Since His will is that to posterity
Thou shouldst for life and death a pattern be,
And that the world should notice have of this, 525
The purpose and the authority is His.
Thou art the proclamation, and I am
The trumpet at whose voice the people came.

520 second . . . rent *i.e.,* the second annual commemoration
of Elizabeth Drury

DIVINE POEMS

Holy Sonnets

1

Thou hast made me, and shall thy work decay?
Repair me now, for now mine end doth haste;
I run to death, and death meets me as fast,
And all my pleasures are like yesterday.
5 I dare not move my dim eyes any way;
Despair behind and death before doth cast
Such terror, and my feeble flesh doth waste
By sin in it, which it towards hell doth weigh.
Only thou art above, and when towards thee
10 By thy leave I can look, I rise again;
But our old subtle foe so tempteth me
That not one hour myself I can sustain.
Thy grace may wing me to prevent his art
And thou like adamant draw mine iron heart.

2

As due by many titles I resign
Myself to thee, O God; first I was made
By thee and for thee, and when I was decayed,
Thy blood bought that the which before was thine.
5 I am thy son, made with thyself to shine,
Thy servant, whose pains thou hast still repaid,
Thy sheep, thine image, and till I betrayed
Myself, a temple of thy spirit divine.
Why doth the devil then usurp on me?
10 Why doth he steal, nay ravish that's thy right?
Except thou rise and for thine own work fight,
Oh I shall soon despair when I do see

Sonnet 1 13 **wing me** give me wings **prevent** frustrate 14
And if **adamant** a magnet **Sonnet 2** 9 **usurp on** wrongfully
appropriate

That thou lov'st mankind well, yet wilt not choose me,
And Satan hates me, yet is loath to lose me.

5

I am a little world made cunningly
Of elements and an angelic sprite,
But black sin hath betrayed to endless night
My world's both parts, and oh, both parts must die.
You which beyond that heaven which was most high   5
Have found new spheres, and of new lands can write,
Pour new seas in mine eyes that so I might
Drown my world with my weeping earnestly,
Or wash it, if it must be drowned no more.
But oh, it must be burnt! Alas, the fire   10
Of lust and envy have burnt it heretofore
And made it fouler. Let their flames retire,
And burn me, O Lord, with a fiery zeal
Of thee and thy house, which doth in eating heal.

6

This is my play's last scene; here heavens appoint
My pilgrimage's last mile; and my race,
Idly yet quickly run, hath this last pace,
My span's last inch, my minute's latest point;
And gluttonous death will instantly unjoint   5
My body and my soul, and I shall sleep a space;
But my ever-waking part shall see that face
Whose fear already shakes my every joint.
Then, as my soul to heaven, her first seat, takes flight,
And earth-born body in the earth shall dwell,   10
So fall my sins, that all may have their right,
To where they are bred, and would press me—to hell.
Impute me righteous, thus purged of evil,

Sonnet 5   4 both parts *i.e.*, body and spirit   6 new spheres
i.e., those added to the Ptolemaic system by later astronomers
10 burnt *i.e.*, by the fire expected in the end to destroy the
world; cf. Sonnet 7, l. 5   13-14 a fiery zeal . . . eating (from
Psalm lxix. 9: "the zeal of thine house hath eaten me up")
Sonnet 6   3 Idly indolently   7 ever-waking part *i.e.*, the soul
8 whose fear fear of whom   13 Impute me righteous (cf.
Article xi of the XXXIX Articles: "We are accounted righteous
before God, only for the merit of our Lord and Saviour Jesus
Christ by Faith, and not for our own works or deservings")

For thus I leave the world, the flesh, the devil.

7

At the round earth's imagined corners blow
Your trumpets, angels, and arise, arise
From death, you numberless infinities
Of souls, and to your scattered bodies go
5 All whom the flood did, and fire shall o'erthrow,
All whom war, dearth, age, agues, tyrannies,
Despair, law, chance hath slain, and you whose eyes
Shall behold God and never taste death's woe.
But let them sleep, Lord, and me mourn a space,
10 For if above all these my sins abound,
'Tis late to ask abundance of thy grace
When we are there. Here on this lowly ground
Teach me how to repent, for that's as good
As if thou hadst sealed my pardon with thy blood.

9

If poisonous minerals, and if that tree
Whose fruit threw death on else immortal us,
If lecherous goats, if serpents envious
Cannot be damned, alas, why should I be?
5 Why should intent or reason, born in me,
Make sins, else equal, in me more heinous?
And mercy being easy and glorious
To God, in his stern wrath why threatens he?
But who am I that dare dispute with thee?
10 O God, O! of thine only worthy blood
And my tears make a heavenly Lethean flood,
And drown in it my sins' black memory.
That thou remember them, some claim as debt;
I think it mercy if thou wilt forget.

Sonnet 7   2-3 **arise From death** (this idea that the soul dies
with the body and comes to life at the day of judgment is
exceptional in Donne; in Sonnet 6, ll. 7-8, the soul parts from
the body at death and immediately sees God face to face)
7 **you** i.e., the righteous, who are exempt from the penalties
of death   10 **above** more than   Sonnet 9   11 **Lethean** caus-
ing forgetfulness   13 **some claim as debt** (since God can par-
don only those sins he remembers)

10

Death, be not proud, though some have callèd thee
Mighty and dreadful, for thou art not so;
For those whom thou think'st thou dost overthrow
Die not, poor death, nor yet canst thou kill me.
From rest and sleep, which but thy pictures be,   5
Much pleasure—then, from thee much more must flow;
And soonest our best men with thee do go,
Rest of their bones and soul's delivery.
Thou art slave to fate, chance, kings, and desperate men,
And dost with poison, war, and sickness dwell;   10
And poppy or charms can make us sleep as well,
And better than thy stroke. Why swell'st thou then?
One short sleep passed, we wake eternally,
And death shall be no more; death, thou shalt die.

11

Spit in my face, you Jews, and pierce my side,
Buffet and scoff, scourge and crucify me,
For I have sinned and sinned, and only he
Who could do no iniquity hath died.
But by my death cannot be satisfied   5
My sins, which pass the Jews' impiety.
They killed once an inglorious man, but I
Crucify him daily, being now glorified.
Oh let me then his strange love still admire;
Kings pardon, but he bore our punishment.   10
And Jacob came clothed in vile, harsh attire
But to supplant and with gainful intent;
God clothed himself in vile man's flesh that so
He might be weak enough to suffer woe.

Sonnet 10 7 soonest . . . go (the good die young) 8 de-
livery deliverance, release 12 swell'st exult, puff up **Sonnet
11** 5 satisfied atoned for 6 pass surpass 8 being *i.e.*, he
being 9 **admire** wonder at 11 Jacob (who obtained his
father's blessing in the guise of his brother Esau (Genesis
xxvii))

12

Why are we by all creatures waited on?
Why do the prodigal elements supply
Life and food to me, being more pure than I,
Simple, and further from corruptión?
5 Why brook'st thou, ignorant horse, subjectión?
Why dost thou, bull and boar, so sillily
Dissemble weakness and by one man's stroke die,
Whose whole kind you might swallow and feed upon?
Weaker I am, woe is me, and worse than you;
10 You have not sinned, nor need be timorous.
But wonder at a greater wonder, for to us
Created nature doth these things subdue,
But their Creator, whom sin nor nature tied,
For us, his creatures and his foes, hath died.

13

What if this present were the world's last night?
Mark in my heart, O soul, where thou dost dwell,
The picture of Christ crucified, and tell
Whether that countenance can thee affright—
5 Tears in his eyes quench the amazing light,
Blood fills his frowns, which from his pierced head fell.
And can that tongue adjudge thee unto hell,
Which prayed forgiveness for his foes' fierce spite?
No, no! but as in my idolatry
10 I said to all my profane mistresses,
Beauty of pity, foulness only is
A sign of rigor, so I say to thee:
To wicked spirits are horrid shapes assigned;
This beauteous form assures a piteous mind.

14

Batter my heart, three-personed God, for you
As yet but knock, breathe, shine, and seek to mend.

Sonnet 12 4 simple not compounded (and therefore more
durable) 13 tied restricted, bound Sonnet 13 5 amazing
dazzling 11 Beauty of pity *i.e.*, beauty is a sign of pity
foulness ugliness 14 assures (me that Christ has) Sonnet
14 2 mend heal, cure

That I may rise and stand, o'erthrow me and bend
Your force to break, blow, burn, and make me new.
I, like an usurped town to another due,   5
Labor to admit you, but oh, to no end!
Reason, your viceroy in me, me should defend,
But is captíved, and proves weak or untrue.
Yet dearly I love you and would be lovèd fain,
But am betrothed unto your enemy.   10
Divorce me, untie, or break that knot again,
Take me to you, imprison me, for I,
Except you enthrall me, never shall be free,
Nor ever chaste except you ravish me.

18

Show me, dear Christ, thy spouse so bright and clear.
What, is it she which on the other shore
Goes richly painted? or which, robbed and tore,
Laments and mourns in Germany and here?
Sleeps she a thousand, then peeps up one year?   5
Is she self-truth and errs? now new, now outwore?
Doth she, and did she, and shall she evermore
On one, on seven, or on no hill appear?
Dwells she with us, or, like adventuring knights,
First travel we to seek, and then make love?   10
Betray, kind husband, thy spouse to our sights,
And let mine amorous soul court thy mild dove,
Who is most true and pleasing to thee then,
When she is embraced and open to most men.

Good Friday, Riding Westward

1613

Let man's soul be a sphere, and then in this
The intelligence that moves, devotion is;
And as the other spheres by being grown

Sonnet 18   8 one *i.e.*, Mt. Moriah, where Solomon's temple
stood   seven *i.e.*, the seven hills of Rome   2 **intelligence**
angelic spirit guiding a heavenly body (**sphere**)

Subject to foreign motions lose their own,
5 And being by others hurried every day
Scarce in a year their natural form obey,
Pleasure or business, so, our souls admit
For their first mover, and are whirled by it.
Hence is't that I am carried towards the west
10 This day when my soul's form bends toward the east.
There I should see a Sun by rising set,
And by that setting endless day beget;
But that Christ on this cross did rise and fall,
Sin had eternally benighted all.
15 Yet dare I almost be glad I do not see
That spectacle of too much weight for me.
Who sees God's face, that is self life, must die;
What a death were it then to see God die!
It made his own lieutenant, nature, shrink;
20 It made his footstool crack, and the sun wink.
Could I behold those hands which span the poles
And tune all spheres at once, pierced with those holes?
Could I behold that endless height, which is
Zenith to us and our antipodes,
25 Humbled below us? or that blood which is
The seat of all our souls, if not of his,
Made dirt of dust, or that flesh which was worn
By God for his apparel, ragged and torn?
If on these things I durst not look, durst I
30 Upon his miserable mother cast mine eye,
Who was God's partner here, and furnished thus
Half of that sacrifice which ransomed us?
Though these things as I ride be from mine eye,
They are present yet unto my memory,
35 For that looks towards them; and thou look'st towards me,

4 foreign motions *i.e.*, those of other spheres   6 **natural form**
own nature   10 **form** essence   11 **rising** *i.e.*, ascending the
cross   17 (cf. Exodus xxxiii. 20: "Thou canst not see my face:
for there shall no man see me, and live")   20 **wink** close its
eyes   22 **tune** *i.e.*, impart their music to   24 **Zenith** (literally)
point directly overhead   **antipodes** the people who live on the
opposite side of the globe   26 **seat** (whether the seat of the
soul was in the blood was a moot point; therefore, regardless
of whether Christ's soul was seated in his blood, all men's souls
are seated in it (because it was shed for their salvation))

O Saviour, as thou hang'st upon the tree.
I turn my back to thee but to receive
Corrections till thy mercies bid thee leave.
O think me worth thine anger, punish me,
Burn off my rusts and my deformity, 40
Restore thine image so much by thy grace
That thou mayst know me, and I'll turn my face.

A Hymn to Christ

AT THE AUTHOR'S LAST GOING INTO GERMANY

In what torn ship soever I embark,
That ship shall be my emblem of thy ark;
What sea soever swallow me, that flood
Shall be to me an emblem of thy blood.
Though thou with clouds of anger do disguise 5
Thy face, yet through that mask I know those eyes,
    Which, though they turn away sometimes,
        They never will despise.

I sacrifice this island unto thee,
And all whom I loved there, and who loved me; 10
When I have put our seas 'twixt them and me,
Put thou thy sea betwixt my sins and thee.
As the tree's sap doth seek the root below
In winter, in my winter now I go
    Where none but thee, the eternal root 15
        Of true love, I may know.

Nor thou nor thy religion dost control
The amorousness of an harmonious soul,
But thou wouldst have that love thyself. As thou
Art jealous, Lord, so I am jealous now. 20
Thou lov'st not, till from loving more thou free
My soul. Whoever gives, takes liberty.
    O, if thou car'st not whom I love,
        Alas, thou lov'st not me.

38 **Corrections** punishments **leave** stop (punishing) 41 **thine**
image *i.e.*, me ("God created man in his own image")
12 **sea** *i.e.*, blood 17 **control** object to 22 **gives** *i.e.*, gives
liberty

25   Seal then this bill of my divorce to all
     On whom those fainter beams of love did fall;
     Marry those loves which in youth scattered be
     On fame, wit, hopes (false mistresses) to thee.
     Churches are best for prayer that have least light;
30   To see God only, I go out of sight,
          And to 'scape stormy days, I choose
          An everlasting night.

Hymn to God my God, in my Sickness

Since I am coming to that holy room
     Where with thy choir of saints for evermore
I shall be made thy music, as I come
     I tune the instrument here at the door,
5   And what I must do then, think here before.

Whilst my physicians by their love are grown
     Cosmographers, and I their map, who lie
Flat on this bed, that by them may be shown
     That this is my southwest discovery
10   *Per fretum febris*, by these straits to die,

I joy that in these straits I see my west;
     For though their currents yield return to none,
What shall my west hurt me? As west and east
     In all flat maps (and I am one) are one,
15   So death doth touch the resurrectión.

Is the Pacific Sea my home? Or are
     The eastern riches? Is Jerusalem?
Anian and Magellan and Gibraltar,
     All straits, and none but straits, are ways to them,
20   Whether where Japhet dwelt, or Cham or Shem.

9 **southwest discovery** the discovery of the passage to the
Pacific through the Straits of Magellan   10 *Per fretum febris*
through the straits of fever   **to die** (after passing through the
straits that bear his name Magellan died in the Philippines)
16 **home** destination   18 **Anian** Bering Strait   19 **none but
straits** nothing but difficult passages   20 **where Japhet . . .
Shem** *i.e.,* Europe, Africa, or Asia

We think that Paradise and Calvary,
   Christ's cross and Adam's tree, stood in one place.
Look, Lord, and find both Adams met in me;
   As the first Adam's sweat surrounds my face,
   May the last Adam's blood my soul embrace.   25

So in his purple wrapped, receive me, Lord,
   By these his thorns give me his other crown;
And as to others' souls I preached thy word,
   Be this my text, my sermon to mine own:
   Therefore that he may raise, the Lord throws down. 30

A Hymn to God the Father

Wilt thou forgive that sin where I begun,
   Which is my sin though it were done before?
Wilt thou forgive those sins through which I run,
   And do them still, though still I do deplore?
     When thou hast done, thou hast not done,   5
       For I have more.

Wilt thou forgive that sin by which I have won
   Others to sin, and made my sin their door?
Wilt thou forgive that sin which I did shun
   A year or two, but wallowed in a score?   10
     When thou hast done, thou hast not done,
       For I have more.

I have a sin of fear, that when I have spun
   My last thread, I shall perish on the shore;
Swear by thyself that at my death thy Sun   15
   Shall shine as it shines now, and heretofore;
     And having done that, thou hast done.
       I have no more.

24 **first Adam's sweat** (part of the punishment of his disobedience (Genesis iii. 19)) **surrounds** overspreads 25 **last Adam's** *i.e.,* Christ's 26 **purple** (1) the garments the soldiers put on Christ (Mark xv. 17), (2) blood 1 **where I begun** ("in sin did my mother conceive me") 17 **done** (1) finished, (2) Donne

BIBLIOGRAPHY

❧

EDITIONS

The Poems of John Donne, ed. H. J. C. Grierson, 2 vols. (Oxford, 1912).

The Poems of John Donne, ed. H. J. C. Grierson (Oxford, 1933).

The Complete Poetry and Selected Prose of John Donne, ed. John Hayward, revised ed. (London, 1930).

The Complete Poems of John Donne, ed. R. E. Bennett (Chicago, 1942).

John Donne: The Divine Poems, ed. Helen Gardner (Oxford, 1952).

The Songs and Sonets of John Donne, ed. Theodore Redpath (London, 1956).

CRITICISM

Walton, Izaak, "The Life of Dr. John Donne," *LXXX Sermons Preached by . . . John Donne* (London, 1640); *Lives by Izaak Walton* (Oxford, 1927).

Johnson, Samuel, "Life of Cowley," *The Lives of the English Poets,* Vol. I (London, 1781).

Eliot, T. S., "The Metaphysical Poets," *Homage to John Dryden* (London, 1924); *Selected Essays* (London, 1932).

Legouis, Pierre, *Donne the Craftsman* (Paris, 1928).

Spencer, Theodore, et al., *A Garland for John Donne* (Cambridge, Mass., 1932).

Hughes, Merritt Y., "Kidnapping Donne," *Essays in Criticism, Second Series* (Berkeley, 1934, Univ. of California Publications in English IV).

Bennett, Joan, *Four Metaphysical Poets,* revised ed. (Cambridge, 1953).

White, Helen C., *The Metaphysical Poets* (New York, 1936).

Leishman, J. B., *The Monarch of Wit* (London, 1951).